# A KANGAROO
# IN MY
# SIDEBOARD

## Alan Veale

Cover design by Deeper Blue Marketing & Design Ltd

*For the 'Little Imp' of this story
– my Big Sister Susan –
with love from her Little Brother*

# CONTENTS

# The Sideboard

When I was very young I remember being drawn to a sideboard in the front room. It was as long as my bed and nearly as wide. It was made of solid wood, had a cupboard at each end and a couple of drawers in the middle. Nothing unusual about that. But to a nine year old boy who had just been introduced to C S Lewis's fantasy land of *Narnia,* that sideboard started to look a little different.

I would run my hands over the smooth door panels, and then use my fingers to trace the delicate patterns of raised veneer around the edges. Imagination would take over as I pressed a rounded centrepiece, childish wonder transporting me through the secret panel I so wanted to be there.

It even had its own smell. If I pushed my face against the dark-stained wood I was convinced I could still detect the living, breathing tree from which this "enchanted" piece of furniture had been formed. Imagine my delight when I found it really *did* have a secret compartment! My big sister Susan (six years my senior) once showed me the trick of pulling open the bottom drawer, and then feeling for a ridge underneath that would allow a shallow mid-section to slide out. Unlike the rest of the drawers this part was lined with velvet, so it had to be extra special. I could hardly contain my disappointment when I realised the hidden compartment did not hold an ancient map leading me to nuggets of gold or a secret world, but some musty letters and a few old photographs.

In truth that secret drawer really *was* my personal treasure. Inside that hidden recess was an adventure beyond my imaginings: a story of romance, of new beginnings and the promise of a better life. Here were answers to the questions I had about the parents who made me what I am. Many years later Susan and I returned to look inside that sideboard, and to finally appreciate the epic journey our parents had undergone. What follows is our mother's story, edited from letters and other documents she left behind.

*Alan Veale*

# Mollie's Journal

# Part One

## *The Dream*

Mollie Veale in 1950

*September 1949 – on board SS Esperance Bay, at sea*

My eyes are closed, but I know the sun is out there. I am bathing in such a wonderful blend of light and warmth as I have never felt before. I can hear the sea too, and taste the salt painted on my lips by the strong breeze. This really is living the dream. In a moment I expect to wake up to a dull, rain-soaked day in Manchester with a list of household chores to work through. Or perhaps by some miracle I have already been transported to a tropical island, ready to be waited on hand and foot by dusky natives.

In reality I am seated on a deck chair among a small group of passengers belonging to the *Esperance Bay*, currently steaming her way at about fifteen knots around the coast of Spain. I can allow myself the luxury of day-dreaming, letting my senses pick out the noise of the sea and the strengthening warmth of the morning sun, while my ears have grown accustomed to the steady throb of engines powering the ship south and east on its six week journey. Eric has taken Susan off to play in the children's room, and I am indulging in a spot of relaxation that feels strangely addictive. If this is an indication of how our lives are about to change, then it is more than welcome. Despite the occasional speck of smutty smoke from the funnel landing in my hair, and the familiar childish shrieks in the background, I feel more relaxed than I can remember since our honeymoon. My thoughts start to drift to another set of pleasant memories, but then I have a rude awakening as I feel an object slam against my right shoulder.

'Wake up Mummy!' My little girl has run as fast as her legs will carry her across twenty feet of deck, so it seems she has collided with the wooden framework.

'Oh, Susan! Please be careful!'

Startled by this interruption to my fantasies, I must look

rather peculiar to her, as my reaction produces a fit of giggles from the beaming three year old. I put my arm out to steady her as she jiggles up and down with unrestrained excitement. Then I arch my neck round as another voice interrupts her juvenile chatter.

'Hey, she beat me!' Eric strolls into view. 'I tell you, Mollie, that little thing can certainly run. Calm down, Suey! She's pretty good on the swing too. How did you get on?'

But Susan's needs are urgent: 'I want a chair too, Mummy!'

I pull her onto my lap. 'Oh it was heavenly! If I closed my eyes I could have been on a desert island. Apart from the noisy neighbours, that is.'

'Yes, there are a few others competing for kiddie's facilities, and I suppose they hadn't appreciated Mrs Veale was trying for a nap. Come on then. Let's swap now you're awake. You've got that letter to finish off, haven't you?'

'Can I do my colouring?' A perennial question from my art-obsessed daughter.

'In a minute, Susan!'

Time to give in. My idyll is at an end, and it is clear I will get no sympathy from either of them until I relinquish my throne. 'Eric, you're a cruel man, but a fair one. Yes, I've still got a page and a half to fill, so I'll give Elsie and Alan an update. Yes, Little Imp! You can sit with me and do some more colouring while mummy writes her letter. Don't let this deck chair go, Eric! I might want to try a little more sunbathing when we get back. A girl can get used to this.'

I can sense his eager anticipation while I take hold of Susan and a raffia basket containing handbag, writing paper and pen, drawing materials and a bag of sweets. Eric has a grin on his face as broad as the proverbial Cheshire Cat as we walk off in the direction of the writing room. I can't help smiling at the loud sigh behind me as he finally takes possession of the much-coveted deck chair.

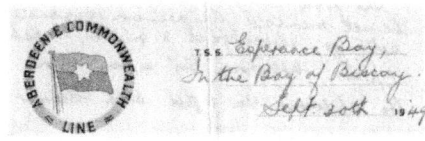

*My dear Elsie & Alan,*

*It is difficult to believe we are in the middle of the ocean. This is a lovely writing room and except for a little vibration and slight roll, we might be sat in a hotel. We had a weary journey to Southampton as we had no breakfast, and had to do some queuing up to give up ration books, customs etc before going on the ship. The journey to London was very good, right on time. We went in a Corner House with Joan and had a good meal. Susan was fascinated with the orchestra and included bands in her prayers that night. We were fixed up alright in Sussex Gardens but had to come away too early for breakfast.*

*The ship sailed about 12.30pm, and we didn't know until it was well out from the dock. We were having lunch and suddenly noticed the land slipping past the portholes! Of course, I didn't bother about pudding and dashed up on deck, but I was glad I had missed the first break as I dreaded it very much. The land soon disappeared as it was misty and has been ever since. It's just sea and mist all round us now. I hope it will clear soon.*

*We are separated. Eric is in another cabin, while Susan and I share with another mother and her little girl aged 5. Last night we couldn't get the kiddies to settle, they both wanted to climb the ladder to the top bunks. We left them finally and took the ladder away, and going back later on the steward said Susan had swung herself down and come out in the corridor saying she wanted to 'wee wee'. However we did eventually get them off and I slept quite well. The bunks are very nice.*

*The food is good too. It seems to be all meals. We are on second sittings, breakfast 8.45am, lunch 1pm, afternoon tea 4pm. Then the children have their tea at 5pm and dinner 7 o'clock.*

*We cannot send any letters until the ship reaches Malta, so have sent you a radio air letter today. We shall reach Adelaide on Nov 5th, all being well of course, so it would be best to write direct to Keith.*

*We shall try and get deck chairs as soon as possible. I've only seen about half a dozen belonging to the ship up to now, and there are 515 people on board.*

I finish reading over the partly completed letter, and feel it is an accurate enough summary of our journey so far. I trained as a shorthand typist after leaving school, and then spent several years working in a busy office in the city before I married Eric, so it has become a habit of mine to check everything I write. Susan is on my lap, happily making patterns with crayons on her own piece of paper, so I adjust my position at the desk and continue writing to my brother and sister-in-law.

*Saturday*

*Beautiful morning. Weather getting warmer. Still a bit misty or we should be able to see the coast of Spain. We played Housey Housey last night, and Eric won 12/2d. What with gambling and cheap drinks (we've had a couple of gin & limes), I'll be a depraved woman by the time we reach Australia.*

*So far I haven't had much time on my hands. We*

*had to queue up a long time for a reserved table on Thursday night, and up to now the kiddies are very restless and unsettled.*

*There is a shop on board which seems to sell practically everything (including nylons, but they haven't released those yet).*

*Susan is sat on my knee drawing weird diagrams, she sends you lots of love and kisses, sticky ones of course. Plenty of chocolate and toffee on board, also Players cigarettes – 2/6 for 50!*

*Will write again soon, Eric has sent you a postcard of the ship.*
*Much love always*

*Mollie*

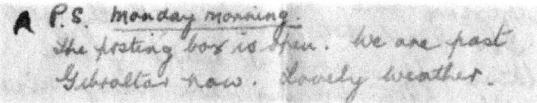

P.S. Monday morning.
The posting box is open. We are past Gibraltar now. Lovely weather.

SS Esperance Bay

My first letter home. Now "home" is wherever I can lay my head. In a few short weeks I will be an Australian Citizen, and settling in to a new home and a new life. Eric and I are joining so many of our kin and pinning our hopes for the future on promises of a better life in another country. A few years ago I could never have imagined taking such a huge gamble, so what has happened to bring me to this?

Curiously it began with another letter. The War had been over barely a year when it arrived. It had travelled twelve thousand miles, and the excitement was obvious on Eric's face as he slit open the envelope.

'News from Hurtle in Australia.'

'Where's that?' I said as I placed our month old baby back in her cot. 'I'm sorry I don't know much about Australia.'

Eric with Hurtle

'It's not a *place*,' he said. 'It's a bloke I knew in Palestine. His name is Hurtle! He was a sapper with ANZAC and we got quite close...'

His voice trailed off while he studied the contents of his letter. Idly I wondered if this Australian soldier had some sort of skin condition. I had no idea then about overseas army divisions. We had just come home from a short walk with our daughter in her pram, and I was thankful that she seemed to be fast asleep. Last night Susan had woken me three times, so now I was more interested in my bed than in Eric's news from abroad. I started to unlace my shoes.

'Listen to this, Mollie!' He was standing in the doorway, reading from his letter. *'Eric, this is a wonderful country if anyone is prepared to work. We had one of my pals and his English bride out here the other week and she could not get over all the fresh butter, cream, eggs, fruit and vegetables we have over here...'*

I listened, but somehow the words weren't making much sense. Where was this wonderful shop?

Then Eric spoke again. 'What do you think?' he asked. 'Be a great place for Susan to grow up.'

I looked at him, realising I was expected to respond with enthusiasm. Hazel eyes sparkled above a broad smile that usually melted my heart. But today was different. Today I lived in a world where a woman needed to be more than a romantic heroine. Today I had to snatch what sleep I could, then put food on our plates, make up a coal fire and soak two soiled nappies.

I took the letter from Eric and chewed my lip in an effort to concentrate as I studied the page. Blue spidery writing on thin blue paper, but some of the words were easy to read: *butter, cream, eggs...* It was a shopping list too far – all of it desirable, but sadly out of reach of my ration book. Then I glanced at the cot by my side in the cramped little bedroom. Only last night we had talked of our concerns for the child's future. Our entire world was here in this one room at the back of my mother's house. Could we dare to dream of something better? I tried to picture us in a different world: our own house, sunshine and three smiling children. But there was a problem with that sort of vision.

'It's a long way away.'

'That's the point!' Eric was not to be dismissed easily. 'Australia hasn't been touched by the war in the way we have. Think about it, Mollie. No rationing! Hundreds of opportunities for work! Hurtle's a good mate. He could help us get settled there.'

I did think about it. I stared back at my husband and tried to remember what I could about Australia. Red portions on a map, or was it pink? I thought back to my schooldays with Miss Travis and a huge globe dominating a corner of the classroom. I remembered her turning it slowly to show us the pink-coloured extent of the British Empire. Canada was the largest single expanse, and then she spun the globe to show us the next in size at the bottom of the world – Australia. We asked lots of questions then: Why didn't they fall off if they lived upside down? What was it like to live in a pink country? *What was it like?* Miss Travis told us it was hot there, and they had natives who threw strange sticks in the air that flew in a circle. The tomboy inside me was desperate to own one of those sticks.

The memory brought the beginnings of a smile to my face which I immediately quashed, not wanting to give Eric any encouragement for an idea which, at first mention, seemed too fantastic to contemplate. Then Susan began to splutter in her sleep, little bubbles of saliva decorating her tiny lips as a growing squeal emerged demanding my milk. It was a welcome distraction for once, and I threw a smile of apology over my shoulder as I started to unbutton my blouse.

'Not now, Eric. We'll talk about it later, shall we?'

It was a topic of conversation that would be raised many more times. While I knew Eric was right to look at alternative prospects to those in Britain after the war, all I could think about was the wrench such a parting would cause. Emotions had been running high enough following my father's death less than a year before. He had been sixty three, and we all felt his loss deeply. Father and Mother had been the same age, and her own poor health was a growing cause for concern. Brothers Alan and Bert were both recently married and living nearby. But my younger sister Joan had moved away to London, and that at first seemed a huge distance to cope with – so the prospect of relocating to a foreign country on the other side of the world was totally unreasonable.

Or was it?

Mollie with Susan 1947

Eric's idea of moving to Australia became an obsession. Each letter we received from Hurtle painted a clear picture of brighter prospects in a new country. The former soldier was now a farmer, but he was looking to change from growing crops to rearing sheep. It seemed the meat market in Australia was booming, and if Hurtle could also buy a butcher's shop he reckoned he would need help with the business side. I was sure it was this that had been the real reason behind Eric's decision to work with his brother-in-law, who ran a butcher's in Chorlton.

At the shop he gained first-hand knowledge of the meagre allowance a housewife had to manage on, struggling to put protein on a plate in an economy that had been restricted for years. I laughed as he finally started to appreciate what life was like from my point of view. Not one to do anything by halves, Eric next announced he was starting a night school course in bookkeeping. He had been a regular soldier since 1935, signing up at the age of twenty one in preference to doing factory work. The army had sheltered him from the real world until a few months before Susan was born, so I couldn't blame him for looking at alternative lifestyles in another country. But convincing me this impossible dream could work for *us* was never going to be easy when I felt so strongly about my immediate family.

One Sunday we boarded a tram on our way home from church in Hulme. Eric carried Susan in his arms as I could not offer her the same degree of protection. A childhood accident had left me with a hip problem and a severe dose of tuberculosis. The result was my left leg grew shorter than my right, leaving me with a pronounced limp. Once I was seated on board Eric was able to hand Susan back to me, before drawing my attention to a poster opposite that had been left up too long after the event: *Let us Face the Future* – the rallying call from Attlee's Labour Party manifesto.

'See that?' said Eric. 'The promises we were made? We

voted them in to change this country for the better. Promised us a major new health service and goodness knows what else. What have we actually got?'

There was no need for me to reply. The answer was all around us: broken fittings and peeling varnish on the wood trims inside the tram, cracked and stained leather on our bench seat. But the real evidence was etched into the faces of the other passengers – pale and drawn, eyes cast down, Sunday-best clothes patched and worn thin as their owners tried to maintain an illusion of prosperity.

Our tram lurched from one side to the other as it rounded the corner into Chorlton Road, a long metallic screech assaulting my ears as the wheels scraped the side of the rails. I clutched Susan tighter to my chest in case her little head should come into contact with the window next to me. She gave a squeal and reached a tiny hand up to try and touch the grimy surface of the glass, streaked with rusty condensation. An older woman in a matching maroon coat and hat sat opposite us, and gave me a disapproving stare as Susan made a further protest. I smiled in apology but got a blank response in return.

The war was supposed to have united us all in fighting for a common cause, but now each of us seemed preoccupied with our own private battles. All of us were struggling to get by day-to-day. Britain no longer seemed so "Great" now that the war was won.

Eric was in conversation with another passenger. The man had been with us that morning at the church service, and I remembered him saying he had recently moved to the area from somewhere near London.

'This country has been pulling together so long it's exhausted,' said the man. 'My cousin and his wife are selling up and moving to Canada. Can't say I blame them. Surely there ought to be a better life for us here after all we've been through? What price Victory, eh?'

I didn't look up, but I could sense Eric glance in my

direction at the mention of Canada, and I desperately tried to think of something more positive to contribute. I used my glove to wipe a clearer patch of glass for Susan to look out at the grey city landscape. In my heart I knew the stranger had a point. Eric and I had been offered a plausible solution and it deserved serious consideration. Perhaps I was behaving like the proverbial kangaroo with my head stuck in the sand. Or was that some other animal?

*October 1949 –*
*on board SS Esperance Bay, past Suez*

It is the first week of October, and Australia is still nearly four weeks away. But this voyage has been like nothing I have ever experienced. Eric reminds me over ten years before he had sailed with five hundred men on a ship very similar to this, but then the home port had been Liverpool. They had taken a similar course through the Med to Port Said, and then taken a shorter journey by train to Palestine for the necessary demands of army service. Now he is able to point out some familiar landmarks to us as we enter an engineering marvel called the Suez Canal. We are almost a quarter of the way to Australia!

The deep rich colours of the sea enthral us all, passing

through turquoise and emerald green to every shade of blue, all governed by the depth of the water below. We are steering a course across the Red Sea to the Arabian Sea and then on to Ceylon, before crossing the equator via the Indian Ocean to reach the western coast of Australia at Fremantle.

Eric has decided to write to his younger sister, Pat – but never considers a letter to his father. My own parents had both been so dear to me, and yet Eric's accounts of childhood are very different to mine. He had been close to his mother, who died suddenly while he was serving overseas, and Pat had only been ten when he left. But he has two brothers and another sister, all now married and with their own children. That doesn't seem so very different to my own background, but then Eric explains it to me in a simple way: 'Your family hugs a lot. Mine just shake hands'.

Now we have a little family of our own, all of us clinging to the ship's rail, and delighting in the experience of warm wind peppered with sea spray. I squeal with delight as I catch sight of a porpoise leaping out of the water just yards from the ship. I haven't felt so happy since our wedding day.

It is very much like a holiday, but one we have never known before. There are so many goods available to us on board – without limit and at cheaper prices – that it immediately puts a brighter gloss on the whole adventure. The gloom of ration-infested Britain is becoming a distant memory. Not only do we not have to pay for, plan or prepare our meals – we have them put in front of us! We can also eat together as a family, and Eric can have a smoke afterwards if he wants, joining other male passengers in the lee of the dining saloon while I and the other mothers take our children off to bed.

The further we travel the higher rises the temperature. After two weeks, as *Esperance Bay* reaches Aden on the

Arabian Coast, peaches in jelly and ice cream with wafers are more than welcome in the stifling heat. Despite it all, I still have thoughts of "home", and keep my promise to write to Elsie and Alan:

*In the Arabian Sea,*
*Sat Oct 15th /49*

*My dear Elsie & Alan,*

*I don't know just where we are at the moment, nor the exact date and am only just beginning to care! The Red Sea seems to have taken all the use out of me. It is cooler now but below decks all the heat seems to be stored up and then of course we are still in the tropics. We went ashore at Aden on Thursday – it was fairly cool in the shade and we enjoyed a wander down the main street looking in the shops. Some of the shops were quite nice and had some lovely things for sale. Eric bought a white silk shirt for 10/- and pyjamas, also white silk, for £1. They seemed to cater for men mostly, as apart from women off the ships, I didn't see any others. There were a lot of beggars, and cheeky little Arab boys. We went in a cafe for iced drinks and suddenly found two little lads cleaning the men's shoes under the table. Eric pushed one off and then we found him attacking Susan's – she wasn't protesting either! She was very good and came all round with us holding tight to my hand, not saying much except when she saw one or two camels and goats. Aden is very hot, dusty with barren looking hills. They haven't had any rain since 1941.*

*The ship took in drinking water. It's terrible stuff because it's treated with chlorine. We are all hoping there will be fresh supplies at Colombo, which we should reach on the 19th. I seem to have been on this ship two months instead of just over two weeks and still three weeks to go. Susan doesn't eat any better. She has had two or three stewards round each threatening, and then when they've gone she says* "He's a nice man isn't he mummy?" *There is a fancy dress party for the kiddies on Tuesday. We are racking our brains what we can do for the imp. At tea time today the steward rashly told the kiddies there would be large balloons for them at the party. So Susan instantly said* "I want a wellow one" *and demanded it forthwith. I asked her tonight* "I wonder what Auntie Elsie and Uncle Alan are doing?" *and she said* "I think they're crying". *So I said* "Why?" *and she answered* "I think they want to see Suey". *So I said* "We'll have to go and see them one day" *and she said* "Yes, we'll go on the bus!!" *Oh dear, I only wish we could.*

*If you leave Knutsford Avenue I wonder if you would put that plant which grew from my wedding bouquet on mother and father's grave. I should like to think of it there. Susan loves the swimming pool. It is lowered for the children for an hour, and Eric takes her in. She doesn't mind the water coming right up to her shoulders now. All three of us slept out under the stars on Tuesday. In the morning we were covered in smuts from the funnel. We are about three hours ahead of your time now so each time I think of you, I have to remember that. I do hope you are both well and that we didn't leave you too much clearing up. It looked dreadful to me. Please give my love to all at Zion, and very much love to both of you.*

*Mollie*

On board *Esperance Bay* (Mollie on RHS)

Eric finishes reading and passes the single sheet of paper back to me on the other side of the table. 'Very good. You write a lovely letter. It's a shame about the ink.'

I glance up from looking in my bag for the envelope I prepared earlier. 'It kept drying up with the heat, I think. What time is it?'

'Nearly ten past nine.'

'Phew!' I fan myself with the envelope and grin at him. 'Gone nine o' clock at night and still so hot out here! I hope the kiddies can sleep.'

Eric smiles. 'She's a nice lady, Mrs Solomons. And Rachel. She and Sue get on very well. They'll probably talk themselves to sleep.'

'Or Mrs Solomons! It's good of her to give us some peace though. I'll miss her once we get to Fremantle.' I look up as a steward approaches our table. 'Eric? Could I have another gin and lime?'

We are sat in the corner of the writing room I had claimed for my own. Eric orders the drinks and gives the steward a ten shilling note, then turns back to me with a wink.

'Depraved woman!'

'Hey! Be careful Eric – I could get used to this. There's still time... Was I right about it being nearly two weeks?'

'Well, it's the fifteenth of October now, and we sailed on the twenty-ninth, so yes – we've had just over sixteen days, and...' he does some mental arithmetic. '...If we keep to schedule we have another three weeks before Adelaide.'

'Gosh! Not even halfway yet.'

We sit quietly for a moment, and then a thought crosses my mind that I just can't shift. I am about to voice my concerns when Eric distracts me with an observation of his own.

'Have you noticed something?'

'What?'

'My asthma. It's gone!'

I stare at him for a moment, trying to recall when I last saw my husband doubled over with the effort of coughing while gasping for breath. He reminds me it had been while carrying our luggage into the cabins on that first day. Over two weeks have passed without incident, and that is the longest asthma-free period either of us can remember since before he was demobbed.

The steward arrives with our drinks before I can reply. 'Oh, thank you. Eric, that's marvellous! What do you think caused it?'

Eric takes the proffered change and places a sixpence tip on the steward's tray. 'Thanks, Sam.' He smiles as he puts the remaining coins back in his wallet. 'The sea air, I should think. We've had plenty of it, after all, and I don't think it matters whether it's humid or not. It's just so much purer than we have at... than we had back in England.'

'But what happens when we get to Australia? What if

you get ill again?'

'I won't. We're going to be arriving at the start of their summer, and that has to mean lots of dry, hot periods. I got plenty of those in Palestine and Persia, and I reckon that sort of atmosphere suits me. So – I think my body will respond to that, and the asthma should get less and less.'

I nod in agreement, although privately I am not convinced. My thoughts drift back to an occasion not much more than a year ago, when I was still struggling to cope with the suggestion I leave my family behind me.

Eric was late. It was nearly seven o'clock and he still wasn't back from work. I knew he should have finished by half past five, and would have no problem catching a tram from Piccadilly. The service was regular, and should have taken no more than thirty minutes, so by now I was getting worried. A loud knock at the door gave me such a fright, and I expected to see a grim-faced policeman stood outside. Instead there was Eric, his hair dishevelled and shirt soaked through, clearly in some distress and supported under the shoulders by two genial gentlemen, both older than him.

'Would you be the lady looking for this young fellow?' asked the shorter of the two.

I must have looked so shocked, but the man seemed oblivious.

'Delighted to meet you, my dear, but your man insisted we bring him here.'

As the three of them eased past me into the hall I realised Eric's breathing was very ragged, and his shirt wet from perspiration. He leaned against the wall and smiled in gratitude at his companions.

'Now you take it easy, Rick,' said the shorter man. 'Your lovely lady will have you right as rain in no time. It's been a pleasure. What a story to tell the grand kids, eh? Goodnight and God Bless.'

With that the two of them nodded to me politely, the short man tipping the brim of his hat as he closed the door behind him. I never found out the names of those Good Samaritans.

Eric's asthma problems began in the army while he was overseas. An accident in a vehicle had broken his nose and surgery had been attempted in field conditions without proper facilities. That was the end of his overseas service and, while his nose seemed to heal, Eric was susceptible to colds and bronchial problems for at least the next two years. Once discharged from the army he did improve with time, but certain conditions could still trigger an asthma attack.

On this occasion he had been slightly later than usual leaving the office, which caused him to run across Piccadilly Gardens to catch the tram. He boarded one just as it set off, but his breathing had become so laboured that he collapsed straight on to the platform. Help was immediately to hand, but Eric could hardly speak, and no one could initially understand whereabouts he wanted to get off the tram. While the short man had suggested they take him to a doctor's surgery in Stretford, Eric had been adamant he wanted to go straight home – and so they had ended up walking a very slow mile and a half to our house in Chorlton.

Ironically, that same day of the asthma attack we received another little blue letter from Australia. Hurtle's ambition to become a sheep farmer was now realised, and so the pressure was back on Eric to consider his business proposition. It was amazing how quickly my husband's breathing got back under control when he opened that letter. I took the opportunity to suggest he fetch some coal in from the bunker outside.


*October 1949 – on board SS Esperance Bay, the equator*

We both agree it is the strangest sight we have ever seen.

Susan is sat on the knee of a bare-chested man wearing a long flowing beard, a cardboard crown and various silk scarves attached to his belt around a very substantial waist. The broom-handle at his side has a three-pronged fork that is probably made from plywood attached atop of it, and this peculiar figure is sat amid a group of other men, some of whom have adopted coconut brassieres to wear over their bare chests, while their lower halves are largely covered by skirts made out of straw.

It is mayhem on a scale neither of us have encountered before. Even Eric with over ten years service in the army says he cannot believe the sheer lunacy of the occasion. We are five hundred souls crammed into every conceivable space in and above the aft sun deck. Many of the more agile passengers have climbed onto deckhouse roofs in a manner that would normally have earned a rebuke from a ship's officer. But not today!

*Esperance Bay* is a jungle of steel with huge metal hawsers and derricks for loading cargo – and limited deck space. Everything seems hot to the touch unless it's in shadow. On a normal day we would have nothing more energetic to think about than scrambling for a prized deck chair, or trying to stop our three year old from throwing herself into the sea. Today it seems more like the rush hour in Manchester, competing for a seat on the tram. We make Susan cling tightly to both of us as we push her through to that portion of the sun deck where a table has been moved from the saloon, and is now smothered by a merchant navy flag together with several boxes and buckets. Those same crew members who might have admonished dangerous practice from a passenger are mingled among us, some perched precariously near the rails, and many of them in costume.

Each of us are awaiting "Examination by the Court of King Neptune" in the sweltering heat just before noon. We have reached Latitude 000000 (the very middle of our world) at Longitude 86 degrees and 28 minutes East of Greenwich. There is nothing physical to show for it (Susan was disappointed not to see a broad stripe crossing the ocean), so we have to rely on what we are told by the crew. One of them has daubed his face in outlandish clown make-up complimented with a red fluffy wig. Apart from a crudely fashioned "medallion" hanging round his neck, his only other attire is what I can best describe as a loin cloth, and he starts the ceremony with a proclamation:

'Hear Ye, Hear Ye, Hear Ye! My name is Davy Jones and you are attending the Court of King Neptune! I hear tell that today we have a large number of Pollywogs wishing to cross the line with the permission of His Majestic Loveliness. But first, will all previously ordained Shellbacks make themselves known?'

For a moment I am struck with a peculiar thought: *we are about to cross a line.* That invisible barrier takes me back to a time when I felt under so much pressure to make a decision. It was a choice I did not want to make and I was starting to panic. For the first time in four years of marriage I was beginning to realise my husband and I were looking at different visions of the future. We were arguing over trivial things, snapping and point-scoring – each of us seeking to reach the moral high ground. Both of us knew the real problem lay in this dilemma over Australia, and the more I resisted Eric's arguments, the more I remembered my dying mother's advice about a wife needing to support her husband. I needed reassurance from somebody, and it came from a surprising direction:

My sister has always been generous, in her nature and with her money. I wrote to Joan one week and briefly mentioned how Susan was getting so big she was now outgrowing her pram. So I was delighted when a brand new pushchair was delivered to our door. A few days later Joan herself arrived for a weekend break, and the weather was kind enough for us to try out our new gift on a special expedition personal to us both.

There was only a slight wind to send a sprinkling of fallen leaves scuttling along the path in front of us. We were on Barlow Moor Road, squinting in bright sunshine as a field of headstones came into view on our left hand side. It was Joan's first visit to our parents' grave in twelve months. I was wearing my winter coat, but wished I'd followed my sister's example by not buttoning it up as the effort of pushing Susan over the distance of a mile was making me quite warm. Joan strode out on long legs, and I had to remind her I didn't have the physique to keep up the same pace.

'Oh, sorry! Would you like me to push for a while?'

'Yes please,' I said. 'Here, I'll take the basket.'

Joan seemed pleased to take charge of steering her niece along the path, and I took the opportunity to examine the small floral arrangement inside her basket.

'Lilac and yellow – Mother's favourite colours.'

'Yes,' said Joan. 'Winter pansies, and the florist found me just the right little pot for them. She'd be pleased, don't you think?'

I smiled, and nodded my agreement. Surely today would be a good occasion to air the thoughts and doubts that kept whirling round my head? I was just about to broach the subject of Australia when we reached the imposing entrance to Southern Cemetery and turned in past the lodge.

'Still no gates,' said Joan.

'No,' I replied. 'Can you remember what the old ones looked like?'

Entrance to Southern Cemetery

'Not really. Sort of Gothic? Black painted metal, I suppose. They've probably found a new home as a pile of shrapnel somewhere over Germany.'

'That would be poetic licence, wouldn't it? Bombed by something that once stood guard in front of a cemetery.'

Neither of us laughed. Neither of us smiled. We both recognised this bit of black humour was only a mask. We were moments away from reaching the grave, and the memory of our mother's passing was still as fresh to us as last week's heavy rainfall.

We took a path to the left, and then steered the pushchair over grass-covered verges and past stone-edged plots towards the latest in a line of white and grey monuments, each standing in silent tribute to the memory of those lying beneath.

Mother had died eighteen months before, and as we approached the now familiar stone cross that marked our parents' grave I found myself feeling apprehensive. Mother and Father had always been full of warmth and love, rarely needing to admonish their children, so I couldn't understand the conflicting emotions within me. I desperately missed their presence in my life, and attending the place where they were now both at rest had previously given me a sense of spiritual peace. Not so today.

'I think she's fallen asleep.'

'What?' I had been staring blankly at the inscription on the headstone. Now I turned my head and saw my sister peering over the top of the pushchair. Susan was slumped over to one side, her long chubby legs dangling on the edge of the step.

'Just look at her. She likes her mid-morning nap, doesn't she?'

I answered with a nod, busying myself by fetching a small fork and trowel from a brown paper bag stowed in the tray underneath. I could feel Joan's eyes on my back as I knelt down and started to tidy the gravel garden bed in front of the headstone.

'Did Eric say anything about the stuff I brought back from London?'

I paused for a moment, my mind returning to the subject I had tried to push to the back of my mind.

'Oh. Yes, he did. He was very grateful. He said to thank you for taking the trouble to call on his behalf. It was very informative.'

'And?' Joan knelt down opposite me and began to pull up some of the growth by hand. 'Did any of it make a difference?'

I considered the question before continuing to fork over the mixture of gravel and soil. 'Well, for one thing we now know Australia House have pretty strict requirements for new migrants, as they call them, to be medically very fit.'

Joan raised an eyebrow but said nothing as I turned my attention to the weed-strewn gravel. The literature on emigration to Australia had been eagerly awaited by Eric, but less so in my case. I had an overwhelming urge to take out my frustrations on the untidy mess in front of me, hardly conscious of the amount spilling outside the plot and onto my coat.

'I mean, look at us! First there's my history of TB, and then there's that business with my heart. Remember what the doctor said when I was in labour?' The burst of energy subsided, and I looked round for the paper bag. 'No, I reckon the Aussies would turn me down flat.'

Joan put some of the uprooted greenery into the bag and passed it to me. 'So what about Eric? What about his asthma?'

'Ah! According to Eric, it shouldn't be a problem. He reckons it's the damp and the cold that make it worse, so a hot country like Australia should be better for him. A lot better. He says they'd take all that into consideration.'

Even as I said it I knew I was in denial. A part of me felt certain Eric must be wrong. How on earth could two people with such obvious physical problems pass a medical in such circumstances? But another part of me didn't want to face rejection on those grounds because I knew Eric wanted it so much.

I stood up and walked over to the pushchair, glanced at my sleeping daughter and then picked up the little floral arrangement from the basket. As I did so I became aware of the peaceful nature of our surroundings, and it seemed to me a hundred souls were now awake and listening to our every word. I stood hesitating in front of our parents' grave, holding the bouquet of lilac and yellow flowers like a jilted bride before the altar.

'I don't know what to do, Joan. I really don't.' I blinked in exasperation, knowing I was close to tears. 'I know Eric's right, and we could do better over there. He would have a healthier life, and I don't want Susan to miss out. But is it right to take her away from the rest of her family? It's not like we're just going to hop on a train! What do you think I should do? I've talked to Alan and to Bert, and they just say it's up to me. Why does it always have to be *my* decision?'

I looked at my sister. We were almost ten years apart in

age, and at least six inches different in height, but we had always been spiritually close. The day she had moved to London had been hard enough to bear, and I wondered how we would manage that physical distance between us. Now I had to consider something much worse – and I was desperate to avoid making a choice.

Joan gently took the flowers out of my hands and placed them on the tidied plot in front of the headstone. Then she stepped into place next to me and linked arms, both of us with our heads bent in respect. A fresh breeze blew some russet-tinged leaves onto the newly tended gravel bed.

'Eric might be right,' she whispered. Then she spoke louder. 'Or he might be wrong – about the asthma, I mean. I do think his motives are right, and I'm sure he is simply looking for the best way to bring up his family. It shows how much he cares.' We were both silent for a moment, and then Joan turned her head and looked down at me.

'Did you study Marlowe at school?'

'Yes, I think so. *Dr Faustus*?'

'That's right. I thought it was dreadfully boring then, but I actually saw a riveting performance on stage at the Old Vic last week. You probably won't remember but it starts with a soliloquy where the good doctor ponders his fate and decides it's not in his control. I quote: *Que sera, sera. What will be, shall be.* Now I'm not suggesting you go and sign up with the Devil, but I do think you should just let fate run its course.' She paused, and I glanced back at our parents' headstone as Joan continued. 'I like Eric. And I love *you*! Why not take the medical? What harm can it do? It takes the decision out of your hands and leaves it with the Almighty. *Que sera?*'

I looked up and saw my own pain reflected in Joan's eyes. But it felt like a cloud had lifted.

It took months for our application to be processed – far longer than either of us had expected. I could see Eric was getting nervous, and it reached a point where neither of us wanted to mention the 'A' word... When the day came, and two identical brown envelopes dropped through the letterbox, my medical report was not what I had expected. 'A1?' Eric nodded and smiled. 'Me too. *A clean report with no major issues.* So – that's it. We've got the "all clear"! Mollie, look at me... You are happy about this, aren't you? It's a chance we can't afford to throw away. You do agree?' I did agree, although with reluctance. The Almighty had dealt the cards and Eric had picked up the winning hand. Now all I could do was to hope his gamble paid off. As the weeks passed and spring gave way to summer, I even found myself warming to the idea of a fresh start. No more dreary wet winters. No more struggling to get a fire going to dry our damp clothing. One part of my brain became fixated with the vision of escaping from all the drudgery of post-war Britain. The rest of it was kept busy with the business of being a wife and mother, as well as with the preparations for emigrating. Alan and Elsie in particular were amazing in all their practical support, readily taking their niece for a short time when I needed help for any reason. Life as a British citizen was rapidly drawing to a close, and yet my marriage to Eric seemed strengthened as we found a new excitement, looking to our future together.

So we crossed a line we had drawn for ourselves, and months later we are genuinely enjoying our new status as *Pollywogs*, queuing up with most of the *Esperance Bay's* passengers who are crossing the equator for the first time. We are required to perform or endure a form of ceremony that often involves water, stepping over or under a cane held by two crew members, or reciting a silly rhyme. After Eric is encouraged to try limbo dancing by two dusky "mermaids" (accompanied by raucous laughter), I am relieved when I am allowed to simply walk under the same pole while keeping a firm hold of our daughter. Each of the children are then introduced to King Neptune before being presented with a certificate in very grand style (signed by "Neptunus Rex") proclaiming each one to be a *Shellback*. Susan makes sure that mummy puts her souvenir safely away in her basket before both of us return to our cabin for some well-earned rest.

Sitting alone with Eric later that day, and without the distraction of our daughter getting in the way, I recall what has been nagging me since we left Southampton.

'Eric, how do we know Mother's sideboard is on the ship?'

He frowns as he considers the question. 'Well... it must be! The paperwork confirmed it would be travelling with us, so it'll be in the hold.'

I am not to be placated easily. 'Yes, but how do we *know* it is? Have you asked anyone?'

Eric sighs. The look on his face tells me I don't need to say any more, as he looks round to attract the steward's attention. Perhaps I should explain about the sideboard.

Susan's third birthday in June heralded an intense period of activity. Our house was back on the market, and plans were made to move in with Elsie and Alan in Stretford until the Big Day arrived at the end of September. First there was furniture to be sold or disposed of.

'It's all just utility stuff, anyway, so I don't suppose we'll get much for it,' I said. 'But not Mother's sideboard. That's coming with us. And my sewing machine.'

'What? It will cost us a fortune to ship that to Australia!'

I played dumb for a moment. 'Don't be silly. It will save us a fortune if I can run up a few items for Susan. I wonder what the price of material is like over there? No, Eric – Mother left that sideboard to me, and it's an antique. Been in her family forever, so I'm not parting with it. Whatever it costs, it's coming with us. It's all I've got left of her, so don't argue.'

Eric said nothing. We had been married five years and he knew when an argument was a lost cause. It was rare for us to disagree anyway, and he always gave way to me on the subject of money. My husband might be a bookkeeper at work, but today was Sunday and he had to acknowledge Home Rule! Eric turned his attention to the pre-embarkation booklet that had just arrived from Australia House that morning.

'This sounds promising, Mollie: *Emigration to Australia*

*in this age is as simple as taking the tube from Blackfriars to Westminster. The emigrant ships are fast, comfortable liners with all modern conveniences, making the voyage through the tropics and foreign seas a rest holiday.* Sounds good. And it's just given me another idea. How about you and me taking a few days off and visiting your sister in London? Joan's got a spare room, hasn't she?'

I'd been kneeling in front of the sideboard, sorting through the contents of one of the drawers. My face must have been a picture as my mouth dropped open, and I turned to stare at my lovely husband.

It was such an inspired idea. What a marvellous opportunity to take one last look around the capital, especially with Joan. Then a snag occurred to me. 'What about Susan?'

'I thought of that. Elsie could have her for a few days. You know she loves that little imp to pieces!'

I smiled at a recent memory of our daughter on my sister-in-law's lap, chuckling at her blowing raspberries. As Eric grinned back at me I knew we shared the same thought.

'You're right. I'll call round there later tonight, and I'll write to Joan in the morning. I haven't seen anything of London for years. Do you know something? I think my hubby deserves a full ration of liver tonight for that idea!'

I laughed as Eric's face lit up with obvious pleasure. How easy it was to reward my man. I replaced my sewing tin in the drawer as another thought struck me: perhaps we could stretch to an onion to go with that liver?

The house sold easier than expected, but Eric and I did manage to fit in our short break to London. Removal to our temporary home in Stretford took place at the end of the second week in September, as Eric left his employment in Piccadilly. Joan, Susan and I then went to a favourite haunt in North Wales for a short break together while the final packing (and re-packing) was done between Eric, Elsie and

Alan.

On the morning of the twenty eighth of September two black taxi cabs were lined up in the street – one for the luggage – their drivers waiting patiently as the final goodbyes took place. I stood at the doorway of our old house in Knutsford Avenue with a lump in my throat I was convinced must be my own heart. All that was once familiar now felt strange. This house had been my home. Now I didn't have one.

Eric stood just outside the porch, ready to steer our little family down the path on the first leg of our long, long journey. The awful moment had finally arrived. We were leaving almost everything we had ever known behind us. Who knew if we might ever return? I stared at my sister-in-law's face, struggling to find the right words.

The Family Home

'I'll write.'

I didn't know what else to say.

'You'd better!' was the reply. 'So will I.'

Elsie was trying to hold her niece in her arms as well as giving me a hug. Big brother Alan stood at her side, his face sombre, waiting to offer affection or support in equal measure. It was the moment we had all been dreading, but we had survived the War, hadn't we? This was     not the end of the world. It was the beginning of a new one.

'Here,' said Elsie. 'You'd better hang on to this one. Take care of each other.'

We walked down to the gate. As we reached it Susan let go of my hand and went running back to her aunt.

'I'm coming back for you Auntie Elsie!'

We stood there, determined to keep the tears in check as my brother gently steered our daughter back down the path, and then all three of us were finally inside the cab. Moments later, the two vehicles moved off in convoy towards the junction fifty yards away.

Inside the second taxi, I hugged Susan tight and squeezed my husband's hand. In my head was a solitary thought: *We're starting a new life, so why does this feel like a funeral cortège?*

But there was no going back. Eric and I were convinced we had done the right thing by putting faith in each other – and in the promise of what Australia could provide for our young family. It hurt me to leave so much behind, but what lay ahead was far more important.


*October 1949 – on board SS Esperance Bay, South Indian Ocean*


We are standing at the stern rail, watching the sea churn up in a white frenzy that marks a chalk-like pathway across the Indian Ocean. The footprint of our progress narrows and disappears in the distance towards a barely defined horizon, sky and sea melting into each other in a heavenly blue. Eric recalls a previous occasion when he observed a similar sight, and once voiced concerns about the threat of submarines following their wake.

'You're dead right there, chum,' says a voice close behind us. 'My brother saw it happen to an escort back in forty three.'

We turn and recognise a fellow passenger; one we have not spoken to until now. He is probably twice our age but very slim, and stubbornly wearing a dark suit and hat during the day while Eric has been in shirt sleeves for most of the voyage. He has just lit a cigarette and now leans back against the deckhouse, inviting relaxed conversation.

'Too many good men were victims of that kind of cowardly attack,' says the stranger. 'Thank God we can put those days behind us.'

'Was your brother in the Merchants, then?' says Eric.

Recognising the men are about to share war stories, I make my excuses and steer Susan in the direction of the children's room. It is a small space and filled with almost all the kiddies on board except Rachel, so with an apology to my daughter that mummy has a headache we come out again and I manage to pull a deck chair into some shade. It is one that most people avoid because the canvas is heavily stained, and the framework only partially repaired after a previous break. Sitting in it is always risky, but I want fresh air as the interior of the ship is so humid and stuffy.

Susan doesn't protest and climbs on my lap for a welcome cuddle while we wait for Daddy to finish his chat. 'Who is that man, Mummy?'

'Which man, darling?'

'The black man talking to Daddy,' says Susan, her thumb slipping back into her mouth.

Realising she must mean the older man in the dark suit I look up, just as I hear the two men approaching.

'We first met in Palestine,' I hear Eric say. 'Hurtle was nearly two years older than me, and two ranks my junior by the time we met up a second time. I made Corporal in December forty one, and about that time we were attending meetings of the Scripture Union together at Bethlehem.'

Both men are smoking now, and as he sees Susan and I cuddled up in our chair Eric nods and drifts towards us. His companion gives me a brief smile out of courtesy, and then carries on the conversation as the men stand in the shade of the nearby saloon. 'That must have been amazing – so you were there for Christmas?'

'We were, yes,' says Eric, warming to his favourite subject. 'Being in Christ's birthplace at Christmas was a big thing for me, especially in the middle of a conflict where peace on earth seemed so out of reach.'

'And Hurtle was there too? You said he was a Sapper? What were the Aussie's doing there?' The man in the suit turns to me with a solemn expression. 'I'm sorry, ma'am. Didn't mean to kidnap your husband. I was just asking him about the gentleman who sponsored you.'

'That's all right. Eric loves an opportunity to talk, don't you, love?'

Eric grins, but for the moment the conversation seems to focus on me.

'You sound like a northern girl!' observes our new friend. 'Or should I say "lass"?'

I laugh. 'That's me! Born in Cheshire but I live in Manchester. At least, we did...' I look down at Susan, who has her eyes closed and her thumb tucked safely inside her mouth. I look up again. 'Are you from London?'

The older man nods. 'Croydon originally, but I've lived in Perth nigh on ten years.'

We find he is returning to Australia following a visit to England after learning his brother had died. He needed to sort out the estate before booking a passage back home on this ship. All the other people we have met on board are new migrants, so it is useful for us to speak directly with someone who has already taken the path we are now embarking upon.

'So long as you've got your mind straight on the important matters, you should be alright. Don't let your woman here hold you back.' He winks at me, then turns back to Eric. 'You just need to know Australia's still a young country, and that means there's plenty of room to grow with it. You can't say that about the Old Country, can you?'

Before we part our new friend has one last observation for us.

'Have you noticed the position of the sun? You see how high it is now? Each day from now on it will be lower in the sky, but you'll find it's always over the horizon to the *north*. So your shade is in the south. And at night you'll get used to a new set of stars.'

I nod, recalling an image from an old school book. 'I've heard about the Southern Cross.'

'Forget that. You won't see it this time of year, and it takes a while to pick it out at first. It's not that bright. Thing that makes me laugh is seeing Hercules upside down!'

He is referring to the constellation of Orion, which will still be visible in the north, but with the perspective reversed. That night Eric and I go back on deck and marvel at the clarity of the Milky Way high above us, familiar constellations sliding away behind the ship as we tip over the edge of the world and continue our journey into the unknown.

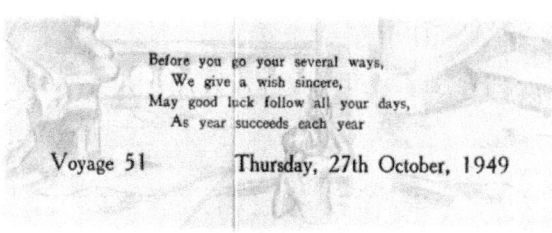

Before you go your several ways,
We give a wish sincere,
May good luck follow all your days,
As year succeeds each year

Voyage 51      Thursday, 27th October, 1949

During the confinement of the voyage we have lived in an alternative world, where the most contentious arguments take place over ownership of deck chairs, and where time often seems to hang suspended in the air like a sundial without a shadow. The journey by ship has been relatively trouble-free. We have barely encountered any rough weather, and the only sickness we have experienced ourselves can be attributed to the heat from the Tropics, rather than the motion of the vessel. Periods of boredom are relieved by episodes of excitement – like the "Crossing the Line" ceremony or the sighting of dolphins. Friendships have been made between passengers and crew, and the convivial atmosphere on board after four weeks is celebrated with a concert and a farewell dinner ("Diner d'Adieu"). The meal is an extravagant affair of five courses, held two days out from arrival in Fremantle, while a "Pommies Parade" concert is organised by the ship's officers, and featuring the passengers as much as possible.

T.S.S. "ESPERANCE BAY"
(Captain T. V. ROBERTS, R.D., R.N.R.)

## CONCERT

Held in the DINING SALOON at 9 p.m.
on FRIDAY, 28th OCTOBER, 1949
AT SEA

Aberdeen & Commonwealth Line

We dock early on the morning of Saturday the twenty ninth of October – exactly one month after leaving Southampton – and so it is a time for parting. I say goodbye to our cabin companions, Mrs Solomons and her daughter, who are to join estranged members of their own family and prepare for their first experience of Australia. For us it is a unique opportunity to sample our adopted home, as *Esperance Bay* is not due to leave port again for another three days.

I am impressed.

*2nd November '49*

*Dear Elsie and Alan,*

*We have just left Fremantle and are heading for Adelaide. We got to Fremantle early Saturday morning and sailed again about 6.30 yesterday evening, so we have had nearly 4 days to go ashore.*

*Well my first impressions are quite good. Firstly the climate is beautiful. Of course I expect it will be very hot soon, but just now in the late Spring the sun is hot but in the shade it is cold and the air is so clean and dry. Fremantle reminds me of a Wild Western town seen on the films, not as bad of course because there are some very nice shops and two very modern cinemas.*

*The first thing we did was to go in a cafe and have a cup of tea with fresh milk and some very luscious sponge cake thick with fresh cream. Susan didn't need any persuasion! Nor does she with the ice cream, she won't eat the ship's ice cream now as it is the English variety.*

*On Sunday we went to Perth which is a beautiful place, there is a nice park, the sea and the river, and on the way back stopped at a small beach. The sand was quite white, and there were men called Life Savers who watch for anyone in difficulty in the sea. They also keep a look out for sharks and there was a tower built especially for that purpose.*

On the banks of the Swan River, Perth

*On Monday we went to Perth again (it takes about 40 minutes on the bus, 1/9 return) and looked at the shops which are magnificent. We spent a long time looking at the food shops alone!! On the whole prices are about the same as England. Some things are much cheaper and some dearer, but there is such variety and a lot of things we never see at home. And of course no Purchase Tax so I think living here should be cheaper. Coats, shoes and dresses are quite good quality and there are loads of lovely materials.*

*Most of the Australian girls and women are very smart, and everybody very friendly. There are girl conductresses on the buses who look more like cinema ushers. I didn't care for the countryside much. To me it is "scrubby". The gum trees have a grey look and the ground is dry and stony, the grass rather brown and coarse. There are a lot of water fountains playing on the grass in gardens and parks.*

*Monday afternoon we went to the zoo at Perth. It is in the open air and Susan had a marvellous time. She was very thrilled with a talking parrot. There are some lovely houses, brick and wood, all detached and nearly all one storey. There are also some very 'seedy' ones especially just outside Fremantle.*

*We had a wire from Hurtle on Saturday saying he is meeting us on the 5th and confirming accommodation is arranged. Oh I shall be glad to get off. It would be nice without children, but all the mothers agree it is a strain with them. Nearly all the kiddies have had something – spots and boils, or fever and a touch of dysentery. Susan has had the latter and been very cross, but is much better now.*

*We are all busy getting ready for packing up. Will write again as soon as possible after we land, but may be delayed as we are sure to be busy for a few days. We have had some rough chilly weather this last fortnight whilst at sea. The ship is rolling a lot and a wave came through our porthole this morning and hit me in the back! Susan said it was naughty and why didn't I smack it!*
*With much love,*

*Mollie*

Nearing Adelaide, November 4th 1949

*5th November 1949 – Adelaide S.A.*

An information sheet in our cabin tells me *Esperance Bay* weighs fourteen thousand tons, and is five hundred and forty nine feet long – so she is not a large ship. It is Saturday morning and nearly two hundred of us are jostling to find a space in what is available to passengers along her starboard side. Our last breakfast on board ship has been served and cleared away, but food is not uppermost in our minds. This is our first proper look at the gateway to a new life in the Promised Land.

Most of us had still been asleep when our ship followed its course north of Kangaroo Island and reached the sheltered waters of Gulf St Vincent. Eric was one of the exceptions. He dressed early and joined a couple of the crew to watch our course in the hour before dawn. He told me later how different it was from our arrival in Fremantle, where even in the early morning we were struck by the vivid colours of the shallow sea and the land beyond. The only hint of colour this time came in the form of blinking navigation lights, and a dull yellow haze near the horizon fifty or so miles ahead.

When Susan and I tumble on deck we are greeted by blustery winds and scudding clouds. We are rewarded with a glimpse of distant hills shaded tan and copper, sheltering behind a shoreline that speaks of little boxes of humanity, some taller than others. The offshore winds this morning also bring a light dusting of drizzle, reminding us of shores we have left behind. Ahead lies a land of opportunity that offers so much – and like greyhounds before the gate we are impatient for the start.

It takes a little over an hour to reach our first stop in Adelaide – the Baggage Hall queue. All disembarking passengers have been standing impatiently on deck for nearly forty minutes before a stern-looking official beckons the first to descend the gangway, personal luggage and raincoats included, eager to become land-based citizens again after over a month on board ship.

'Will Hurtle be meeting us here?' I ask as we wait for the queue to shuffle a further four paces forward.

Eric shakes his head. 'No, not here. He said he'd find us once we'd completed all the immigration procedures. You saw what it said on the pamphlet they gave us last night. After the baggage check we have to go through the medical. Then we have to surrender the passport.'

'Oh, yes... That's when it gets really serious. Do you think there's a chance one of us might fail this time? They might put me straight back on the ship!'

The remark makes Eric wince. 'Don't!' he says.

I am only half-joking, as it seems to me the voyage has gone very well, and surely emigrating is not meant to be so easy? I hear some raised voices ahead of us, deep in another part of the building, and imagine some poor souls being hauled away. Would we receive such harsh treatment? I tighten my grip on Susan's hand and try to peer over our neighbour's shoulder towards the distant doorway.

We amble forward a few feet more, and after a moment Eric tries to lighten the tone. 'It's quite an ancient procedure really. An Arab chap in Palestine told me the Romans started all these immigration checks. They didn't put walls round their cities to keep out invaders, you know. Anyone knocking on their gates with a dose of the measles would get killed on the spot.'

'Eric!' My elbow in his ribs is probably not what he expected. It isn't his best attempt at calming frayed nerves, and I am about to rebuke him further when a fresh voice joins the conversation.

'Welcome to South Australia!'

We look round to see a pink-faced young woman with blonde hair, wearing a smart two-piece suit in olive green, and carrying a clipboard. She has just pushed her way through the crush of bodies in front of us, and now commands attention in the confines of the narrow passage that is our present and only experience of our host country thus far.

'Hello. My name is Lucy. Can I have your names, please?'

Lucy checks her list and ticks off the required confirmation halfway down the second page she carries, then proceeds to reel off a list of instructions regarding baggage checks, customs declarations and medical procedures we are shortly to experience before being directed to our next destination. A similarly dressed girl with brown bobbed hair leapfrogs from a position further up the queue, nodding to her colleague in passing, and begins an almost identical dialogue with the couple standing behind us.

'So where do we go from here? We have someone meeting us.' I am almost shouting now over the vocal clamour that seems to fill the plain-walled corridor around us.

'From here?' Lucy's voice raises a fraction in volume, but remains courteous and polite. 'We will be transporting you by coach to a hostel for refreshment and accommodation for at least one night. Is your sponsor meeting you?' Eric and I nod. 'So he will have been given instructions to meet you at the hostel, which in your case will be Elder Park, right in the centre of the City. You'll feel right at home there. They've got showers and everything!'

The cheerful Lucy is not wrong. We eventually pass through all the initial stages of becoming New Australians, and find ourselves herded on board a bright green bus that takes us through one of the shorter periods of our long journey. We begin with anonymous warehouses, fuel depots and railway sidings, before continuing on through Adelaide's quieter suburbs to the taller buildings and stone-fronted offices common to every city. All of us have our faces pressed to the windows of the bus. Most seem impressed that Australia has everything to offer that we have left behind – and more besides. I remember the narrow bomb-scarred streets that litter the cities of Manchester, London and Southampton. Here the roads are wider and brighter, the buildings unaffected by damage or dirt, colours somehow more vivid, and the signage more American. Electricity cables thread their way along the route atop tall wooden poles, strung there presumably because it is more economical to create an aerial supply than to break open the earth. There is plenty to attract the eye, and I still feel confident a brighter future is out there for the taking.

# Part Two

## *Keith*

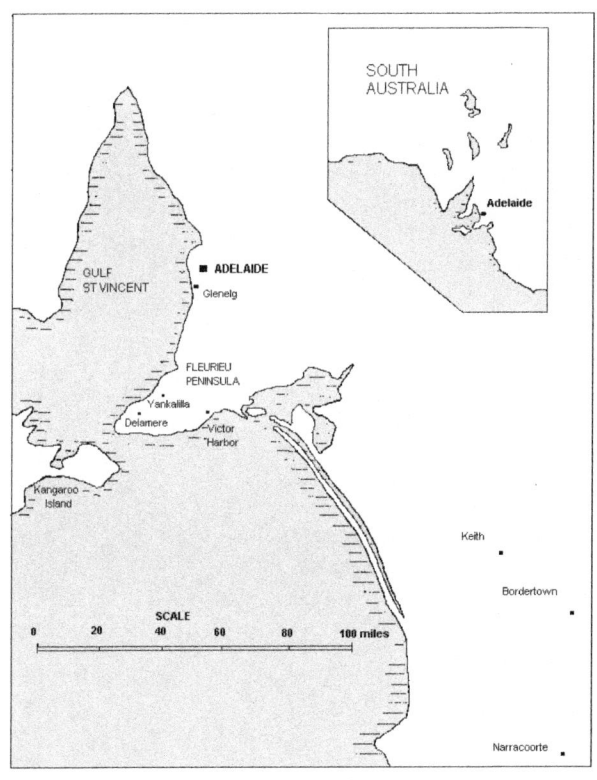

*5$^{th}$ November 1949 – Adelaide*

In the weeks and months before the voyage I would often let my mind drift to distant shores. I imagined myself arriving in a strange land bathed in sunshine, with wide open spaces and bowls of fruit on every table. Eric and I would cuddle up together in a large bed under a single sheet because of the heat, and Susan would sit quietly on the floor, drawing kangaroos – probably from life!

Our first night as Australian residents is not what I expect. On a rather grey Saturday afternoon we are dropped off outside a rambling two storey building that looks to me very much like a government office. We are just three out of thirty two new arrivals to stand in line yet again on that day full of queues and form-filling.

'There he is!'

We are nearly at the reception desk when Eric breaks away to greet a man walking towards us through a doorway marked "Lounge". I see a florid face with an open-necked shirt and a well-worn brown suit. He is below average height but sturdily built, and beaming from ear-to-ear as Eric takes hold of his outstretched hand and shakes it warmly.

Susan and I are still in the line waiting to claim our keys at the hatch, and I am reluctant to give up our place. I don't know if Eric will bring Hurtle over to meet us. Curiously I feel out of place and uncomfortable. It seems for a moment like we are no longer part of the deal. Hurtle never looks in our direction. The two former soldiers are reunited once more, with the women-folk just part of the background.

I glance down at Susan, already pulling me by the hand towards a space vacated by a couple in front, and when I turn my head again Eric is hurrying over to join us – alone.

'He'll catch us up later.'

'Is everything okay?'

'Yes, he's just... He'll let us get sorted out here and call back after we've had something to eat. Come on, we're almost there.'

Over the next half hour we are introduced to our new accommodation: Eric and I are separated again between two plywood-partitioned cubicles similar in size to our cabins on board ship. Then we find our way to a communal dining room where we are given a scalding hot bowl of stew that has been simmering in a pot much longer than it should. At least there is proper cow's milk provided for an industrial-strength pot of tea.

Arrivals at Elder Park Migrant Hostel

I am introduced to Hurtle in the lounge – a large room looking more like a warehouse sale for second-hand furniture, and smelling strongly of cigarettes. Nothing matches, and all of it is well-worn. I think our host looks quite at home there somehow. As we steer our way past several low tables, armchairs and sofas (some of them occupied) I have a better opportunity to study the man who has taken me so far away from my family. Standing to greet us I notice his shoes look scuffed and worn, and the hand he extends towards me has a gold signet ring on the middle finger. His palm feels like old leather.

'G'day, Mollie. Heard a lot about you. Nice little nipper.'

He drops his gaze as I realise the remark is aimed at Susan, shyly clutching a cloth toy and trying to look anywhere other than Hurtle.

'Got two myself. Least that was the count this morning. Got a lot more sheep though...' He gives a dry laugh, but I have the impression good humour is not a ready attribute for our farmer friend. While the mouth forms a kind of smile, his eyes look sad and careworn. It is a different face than I remember from the photos Eric had shown me.

We sit in three armchairs, Susan on my lap, and after a brief exchange of words with Eric, Hurtle stands up again and heads off to the bar to fetch drinks. On his return it doesn't take long for a potential problem to come to light. Our trunk is not yet out of the ship's hold, and we have been told it has to be signed for in person. One official has said it could be at least another day before it reaches us – and tomorrow is Sunday, when everything in the port will be closed. I am adamant I am not leaving the trunk behind. Most of our clothing, toiletries and all of Susan's toys and things are inside. I know I will need those familiar items to help settle my daughter into her new surroundings.

Hurtle nods slowly as he considers the situation. It is an impasse. He cannot afford to miss his train back tonight. We cannot go with him. There is only one solution in his view.

'So here's what you'll have to do: Stay here until your trunk turns up, and then get a train on your own. Shouldn't be a sweat 'cause it's a five minute walk from here. Okay? Train service between here and Keith is by Overland or the Two-Three-One. Two-Three-One doesn't run Tuesdays or Thursdays and your Overland only runs at night. That means getting in to Keith at midnight, like I will tonight. How does that sound?'

It all sounds complex and confusing to me. I am also distracted by Susan wanting to whisper in my ear, so I am grateful when Eric answers for us both. 'I don't think a midnight train will be a good idea, Hurtle. Not with a three year old to consider. And I doubt Grace would be happy if we arrived at that time. So can't we get one during the day?'

'Sure, but only Monday or Wednesday. And it leaves Adelaide about seven in the morning. That way you'll be with us around one o' clock.'

Susan has sensed the slightly strained mood between the adults and is becoming restless, twisting around on my lap and then literally throwing her toy on the floor in a tantrum.

'Susan, that's enough!' I chide the little imp. Then I ease her off my knee and bend down to pick up the toy. 'That does sound better to me, Hurtle. So we'll aim for Monday or Wednesday then. I'm sorry boys, but I'm going to have to get this one to have a lie down on her bed. It's been a long day for her.'

Eric stands up and Hurtle follows suit. 'Hey, I'm bushed too. Look, I'll just show Eric where to catch the train and I'll be off.'

'Oh, right!' says Eric. 'Will you be okay, Mollie? We won't be long.'

But then Hurtle has another suggestion. 'Too right, mate. Like I said, only five minutes from here... Got time for another beer though, if you fancy it?'

Eric turns to me with a questioning look.

'Go on then!' I say. 'But don't expect me to help you find your room when you get back. I'm relying on Susan to find ours as it is...'

I expect the excitement of finally being off the ship will keep me from finding sleep that night, but my pillow is too welcoming, and I wake at seven by someone tugging at my arm. Susan wants the toilet, and I am struggling to remember where I'd last seen it.

In Elder Park

*6ᵗʰ November 1949 – Elder Park, Adelaide*

For the last five weeks we have grown accustomed to eating our breakfast in a dining saloon with a large group of other adults and children. This morning is no different –

apart from the location of the saloon and the variety of food on offer. In fairness, there is nothing wrong with the hostel version; just that there is less choice and we have to help ourselves to most of it. Eric and I both feel hungry, but Susan can only manage three spoonfuls of porridge. I think she is distracted by a little boy on the other side of the table who is wearing glasses so thick they exaggerate the size of his eyes. I am relieved when we finish and I can get her to stop staring.

But the morning finally brings the sunshine, and once a member of the reception staff has confirmed there is no chance of our trunk arriving until Monday, we head outside to explore.

'So what's the lake called?'

We are sat on a bench in a beautiful park within a short walk of the hostel. Another couple we recognise from the ship have stopped to talk to us, and Eric is consulting a pamphlet provided by the reception staff to provide the answer.

'I'm not sure, but this is Elder Park and it says here the lake was formed from the River Torrens,' said Eric. 'Apparently the river used to be clogged with sewage a hundred years ago.'

We all stare at the thirty acre stretch of water in front of us. There is certainly no evidence of its unpleasant history remaining. Apart from its size it reminds me of the Serpentine in London's Hyde Park, with a scattering of swans and ducks dipping and fluttering over a glassy surface. The temperature is rising, and we are surrounded with light and colour. All around us are formal gardens with an abundance of flora and fauna, and a huge bandstand standing in pride of place at the head of a grassy slope.

'Can I have an ice cream?' says a little voice at my elbow.

We laugh at the familiar question, and then agree such a

treat is probably a good idea for us all as the sun climbs higher in the sky. Susan is soon able to confirm Adelaide ice cream is just as good as that from Perth and Fremantle. We even have a second helping later that night during a visit to a nearby cinema. They are showing a series of animated shorts, and we chuckle away happily at the antics of Tom and Jerry and Bugs Bunny. The trunk doesn't materialise until late Monday morning, so all we can do in the meantime is stay around the hostel, or go for short walks in the park. The prolonged stay in the city does at least allow us to explore a little at a comfortable pace, with the hostel providing basic amenities and a last opportunity to socialise with other migrants.

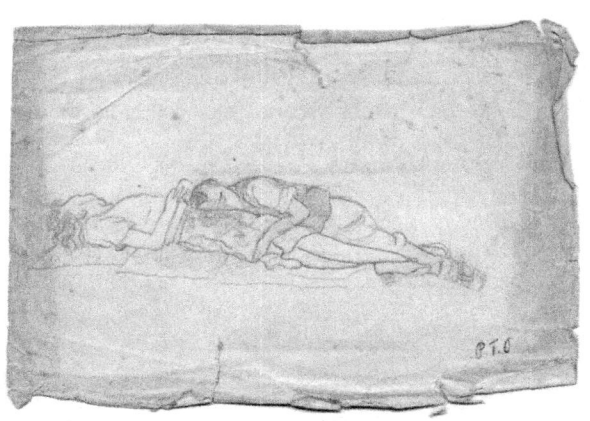

Eric & Mollie Veale resting in Elder Park, Adelaide, Sth Australia, 7th November, 1949.

This sketch was drawn by an art student sitting near to us.

*9ᵗʰ November 1949 – arrival at Keith S.A.*

The final leg of our journey to Keith begins a little after dawn on the Wednesday, as a train made up of five green and cream liveried coaches makes a steady climb through the southern suburbs of the city and heads east towards Melbourne. We stare through the window at the strange sounding names of so many small halts and stations along the way: Balhannah, Coomandook and Tintinara, Petwood, Warla and Tailem Bend. The final stop, and the most English-sounding one of all, will be our ultimate destination – Keith.

After over five hours travel we have grown a little bored of a view from the window that seems to vary so little. The literature Eric picked up at the hostel suggests the enormous expanse of flat earth we have been crossing for the last two hours is termed "mallee-heath". It isn't what I would describe as desert, but a vast stretch of low-lying shrubs clinging to a pale earth that looks parched of water. While the leaves are probably green underneath, they look to be permanently grey with dust, and I feel disappointed that so little of the Australia we have seen so far has any appeal to the eye.

'Penny for them!' said Eric.

I keep my gaze out of the window, as I have just spotted a large shape in the far distance that resembles a ship sinking into the sea. I later learn this is the only mountain in the area, given the name "Mount Monster" by the aborigine population. 'Sorry – I just find this countryside a bit depressing, that's all.'

Eric has Susan on his lap, fast asleep while he gently strokes the strands of brown hair over her ear. 'Are you disappointed? You haven't said much about Australia so far.'

'Well, it's been a bit of a hotchpotch, hasn't it? Adelaide seems nice. Very nice. But this... Well, it's just...

depressing.'

'What about Hurtle? You didn't seem too impressed with him that first day.'

'No. Well, he's your friend, Eric. I need to get to know him a bit more. What's Grace like? I'm probably going to be spending more time with her than with Hurtle. Then there's their children. It's important Susan can get on with them. What are their names again?'

Eric frowns. 'Godfrey and Elaine, I think. No – that's Rita's boy. Could be Geoffrey. I think Grace'll be fine. She's a good bit younger than Hurtle from what I remember. I'm sure you'll get on. She'll probably introduce you to all the women's groups in Keith. You know – there's bound to be plenty of social opportunities for you to... well, socialise.'

I nod and smile. I can't tell Eric how nervous I feel about meeting Grace. I have seen a photograph of her and she looks pleasant enough, but I know very little about her. The letters from Hurtle I have seen rarely mention his wife or children, so I am not at all confident that even Eric has a clear picture of how our new lives are going to shape up. But this isn't the time to be faint-hearted. I sit back and close my eyes, remembering how bright and spacious some of the houses had looked as we travelled through the Adelaide suburbs. Would ours be similar? Hurtle didn't mention anything when we met. I suppose he wanted to keep it a surprise. Months ago Eric told me Hurtle would be building us a new house. New! I tried to picture it in my mind – freshly painted with plenty of space for me to turn into a proper home. But then I feel the train jolt a little and begin to slow. We will soon have our questions answered, as it is time to wake up our sleepy daughter and fetch the luggage from the rack above our heads.

The flow of air that has been an almost constant companion through the open window now deserts us. It is early afternoon, and the heat is oppressive. Our choice of carriage has been a good one, as only the first four are in a position to use the wooden platform for alighting – and we are the only passengers to disembark. Keith railway station is similar to so many of the others we have seen on the journey: simple wooden structures with a single small shelter in the middle for passengers and railway employees to use.

At one end of the platform stands a solitary figure – this time wearing a broad-brimmed hat for protection against the sun. Hurtle has obviously been at work, and as he approaches to help with the cases the impact of a sheep farmer's day is self-evident. An open-neck shirt with the sleeves rolled up to muscular forearms, smeared with grease and numerous dark stains that are repeated liberally down brown corduroy trousers, worn at the knees and with a good many threads pulled at calf level. I find it puzzling that the upper parts on top of his thighs are worn dark and smooth compared to the sides and back.

'G'day!' is the only greeting, as our host hoists our trunk onto one shoulder with relative ease, and strolls back along the platform towards the road that runs alongside. Parked close by to where a series of timbers have been laid to help vehicles cross the tracks is an old Bedford truck with drop-down sides. Eric follows Hurtle's example and heaves the two cases on next to the trunk, before helping me into the cab. Then Susan is lifted in to sit on my lap in the middle between Eric and Hurtle. With a protesting whine and an alarming series of rattles, the engine splutters into life and the final segment of our long journey begins.

The view from our raised position inside the cab is similar to that of the train window. A flat landscape for miles around relieved mainly by scrub, blue gum and acacia trees clinging to the dry earth and belying the impression that the air is sucking out all the moisture. Surely there must be some water hidden beneath the dusty soil? To strengthen that belief we can see occasional evidence of humanity in a scattering of tin-roofed buildings which are all we can see of Keith township. Hurtle notes our silent wonder and makes his own interpretation.

'Beautiful, isn't it? This is the sort of place you can hear yourself think. God's Own Country, Eric. Welcome to His Garden. We've arrived!'

The truck pulls up suddenly, and I have to grab Susan tight as we come close to falling forward into the windscreen. Neither of the men seems to notice, and jump out in unison immediately the engine stumbles to a halt. Eric helps us down from the cab, and then joins Hurtle at the back of the truck to retrieve the trunk and the cases, allowing Susan and I to give our attention to the building in front of us. The house is like others we have seen in our short journey from the railway station: single storey weatherboarding over an L-shaped timber frame with a corrugated metal roof. My first thought is *I bet that's noisy when it rains*, but then I dismiss it, assuming rain is a rarity in Australia. I don't have time to take in anything else as a door springs open and a buxom female figure comes down the path towards us. Grace is young and dark, and wears her hair short like me. She wipes her hands on a floral patterned coverall, giving me a quick appraisal up and down, and then a perfunctory hug.

'Hi, Mollie. It's about time. You're going to love Australia. You too, Susan! I've got two little pals here for you, straight off. C'mon in. We'll get a bite to eat then pack you off to see Gladys.' The formalities over with, she turns on her heels and marches ahead of us up the path. I haven't said a word, but grip Susan's hand tightly and hope for the best.

The family home is newly built. In fact, it is so new it still hasn't been finished. The rooms are more spacious than our home in Chorlton, with wooden floors throughout except for stone tiles in the kitchen. Cosy it isn't, with furniture that looks bulky and uncomfortable, leather on wood. There are just the two bedrooms. None of it has been painted, but Grace is in the middle of applying a coat of lime to the kitchen walls. Something is bubbling away in a huge pan on top of a wood stove, but the lime is disguising the smell. I listen to this young woman explaining the rules on using the fly-screen door, but my thoughts are beginning to stray. Where are we going to sleep? And why does it feel like we are intruding?

I feel the bottom dropping out of my world as I look down at our tired little daughter. Susan is shyly clutching at my skirt; whether for physical support or not, I can't be sure. One thought dominates all others: the growing possibility that all my dreams have blown away into the Australian dust.

### 15th November 1949 – at Hurtle's, Keith

Hurtle has a collie dog called Bob, who takes absolutely no notice of us. I seem to remember someone telling me once that dogs can't see in colour. Everything is black and white to them. I don't know if that really is true, but within days of our arrival at Hurtle's it seems all the colour has been washed out of me. Is this what it means to lead a dog's life?

Our new world is so different from the old. Hurtle would have had Eric out at the sheep farm that very afternoon if I hadn't put my foot down. There is so much to take in: new surroundings, new faces, strange accents, strange names – and the absurd situation of still living out of suitcases even though we have reached our ultimate destination. Once we have shared a meal (some kind of lamb stew) with Grace and her youngest child Lorraine (two years old), we all have to walk a further half mile in the heat of the day to a house owned by Hurtle's sister and brother-in-law. As we get there, Eric's asthma begins to surface – hardly surprising after carrying two heavy cases all that way.

Hurtle has taken the truck and promised to follow later with the luggage, but Eric insists on bringing the suitcases, which is just as well as we are desperate for a change of clothing. Our own new house turns out to be still in the planning stage, so we will just have to make do for now. But no-one says for how long.

The days begin early around five o'clock, as it is cooler for anyone doing manual labour to get a head start as soon as the sun appears over the horizon. So as Eric and Hurtle drive off to the farm, Grace introduces me to women's work. I have absolutely no idea what I have let myself in for, but like a lamb to the slaughter I show willing and try to match my new neighbour's stamina while she teaches me what will be expected on a daily basis.

I suppose the most obvious (and unexpected) difference I note is there is no mains electricity. In Manchester I realise I had it easy: we had lighting and power at the flick of a switch, or by simply putting a plug into a socket on the wall. But in this newly built house in the sticks of South Australia it is kerosene lamps, battery power – and very little else. Nor does water flow from a tap. Again, there is no connection to the mains supply. Rainwater is collected from the roof into a large open tank, then piped to a smaller tank outside. So every drop of water that we need – for drinking, washing or cooking – has to be carried inside and boiled on a wood-burning stove. There isn't even a sink, so no drainage to let out the waste. What we carry in also has to be carried out – and the toilet isn't connected to mains sewage either. On hot days I try not to go because of the stench, but the washhouse isn't much better. And that is where I first find out what gives Australian women good muscles.

'Will that be enough?' I ask Grace as I deliver my third bucket of water for the copper.

'Hardly covering the bottom yet, girl' she replies. 'Got to fill the troughs next, and they take three times as much water. No worries, Mollie! You're doing just fine. And you with that gammy leg and all. Your Eric must be proud of you.'

She gives me a big smile as reward while I take a moment to catch my breath. Then she tosses some more wood on the fire and excuses herself to fetch the linen basket. I have seen the size of it earlier, so I can't complain she's given me the heavier job. Getting the fire going to heat the copper has taken quite a while, and fetching water seems straightforward enough, even if I have slopped more of it on the ground than Grace is happy with. I feel my education in Australian swear words growing apace.

I have so many questions. But then so does Grace. She wants to know what life is like in Britain, and I try to tell her about our home in Chorlton. But every time I explain about how we do things in England I find myself realising how much easier my old life must sound to her. She laughs when I tell her about our weekly dustbin collection.

'No kidding? You just put your waste in a can outside your kitchen and someone carries it away? You need to tell Eric to set something like that up here. They'd snap his hand off.'

Then she shows me where they dispose of their scraps of waste food: by a bush yards away from the house.

'Wild things'll sort that out.'

I don't want to ask, but make a mental note not to let Susan play anywhere near that bush.


*18th November 1949 – Keith*


The two of us are off to bed. A few short weeks ago that would have meant simply climbing the stairs from our living room to our bedroom, but our new life is dramatically different. Now we have a nightly half mile walk from Hurtle's to his sister's slightly larger house.

Gladys and her husband Colin have two children, although the eldest is already a teenager. They also have a spare room that can fit a normal sized bed and a couch that is more than big enough for Susan. The arrangement is temporary but practical, as it means Susan can be safely left in bed at one house while we either have some private time, or continue with the daily chores at the other.

Eric carries a torch, as the transition from daylight through to night is notoriously brief, and street lighting non-existent. It is a remarkable spectacle to watch the sky's changing appearance from a wonderful deep blue to a sparkling black velvet. An army of stars from the southern hemisphere silently takes up position, its vast numbers seeming to reach out and mock our remoteness beneath them on the dusty track. Ahead of us a half moon springs from behind a random cloud that hugs a hidden horizon, its weak light making little impact on the Australian dusk. We have barely spoken since Eric and Hurtle returned from the farm, and I sense my husband's mood. I know there will only be a brief opportunity to speak in private, unless we restrict our conversation to hushed whispers in our hosts' little bedroom.

'So what happened today?'

Eric says nothing. His head is down, seemingly focussed on the part of track that comes under the scrutiny of the torchlight. I wait. I know he is thinking, trying to find the best way of putting his thoughts into words. But when he does speak his choice of words surprises me.

'I think I made a mistake. We shouldn't have done this. I'm sorry.'

I stop walking, open my mouth but can't speak. Eric stops too, and I stand for a moment trying to make out his facial expression in the failing light. Then I find my voice.

'Why are you telling me this now? What happened to you today?'

Eric hesitates again. 'We slaughtered some sheep. Hurtle

loved it. He'd been looking forward to it like it was a holiday.' He swallows hard before continuing. 'I had to... I killed a couple of them the way he showed me, cutting their throats and then bleeding the carcasses. It's... It's awful, Mollie. I wasn't cut out for this. I know Hurtle wants me to be able to do everything he does, but I just can't do it.'

I wait, sensing there is more to come. The moon highlights a hint of moisture in Eric's eyes as he lets the dull beam of the torch scatter randomly around our feet.

'The butchering I think I could manage. Harold taught me a lot at his shop in Manchester, and I'm okay cutting up a carcass, but holding a living animal and then taking its life away is not something I think I could ever get used to.'

I listen, but find I cannot be sympathetic. Something I can no longer control bursts out of me. 'So what do you expect me to say? We've left our families thousands of miles away for this, Eric. You had months, if not years to consider what life was going to be like over here, and Susan and I are supposed to just accept that?'

'No, of course–'

'It's not exactly easy for me either! I have to muck in with Grace. Do you know what we've been doing today? Well, today was wash day. We had to carry *ten* buckets of water to fill three troughs in the washhouse, which is an absolutely filthy place. Then we had to fill about four more for the copper. Then after that it all had to be carried out and thrown away. Do you think that was easy for me? Do you?'

Eric shakes his head and stares dumbly at his feet. It just makes things worse, seeing him look so defeated. I carry on, unable to stop what I started.

'Grace is at it every minute, and she tells me Hurtle had a dizzy turn last week because he just works himself to death. I can't vouch for that but I do think Grace makes work for herself, preparing so many meals every day. She cooks hot meals for dinner and tea and it's always *meat*!'

I am close to hysterical. I have been getting so worked up I am hardly aware I am clenching my fists like a failing boxer. Now I find myself pummelling my husband's chest in frustration. 'Meat! I'm sick of it already! Why can't we have a nice bit of fish for a change?'

Eric is staring at me now, his face stricken, but the floodgates are open and I can't hold back the rest of my hurt.

'And goodness knows when our house is going to be ready. You haven't even *seen* the shop yet! We're going to have to live in two rooms behind it for months on end. What kind of life is that going to be? What about Susan? She has to try and fit in somewhere too – and you promised me this would mean a better life for her, didn't you? Well? Didn't you?'

'Yes, I did!' Eric obviously hasn't anticipated my anger, but he knows better than to argue. He grips my shoulders and I feel a shock at the heat in his hands. 'I'm sorry, Mollie. I got it wrong. Completely wrong. But I will sort things out.'

I snatch a few deep breaths and look to my left. A faint gleam from a solitary lamp by the door to Gladys and Colin's house can be glimpsed through the scrubby undergrowth at the side of their path. Our daughter will be asleep, thankfully oblivious to the pain we are feeling. But she too has been learning how to cope with conflict. Family life for Susan now includes two other children. Hurtle's son Geoffrey is a year older than her, and he is already asserting his pecking order in the household. He is the image of his father – and it is an image I don't like.

Even in the half-light I can see the hurt in my husband's eyes and the moisture on his cheek, and then I realise my own face is damp too. My anger evaporates faster than my tears, and I reach out to embrace the man I have promised to love, honour and obey. How on earth have we found ourselves in this position? As we hug each other tightly and let the tears flow I know it is useless to try and allocate blame. I have accepted Eric's arguments in favour of migration for all the right reasons, and if Eric has been misled then I will just have to stand by him as I promised on our wedding day. We have to find a way through this mess together. So we cling to each other, alone in a strange land, with only a few billion stars for company.

*20<sup>th</sup> November 1949 – Keith*

I have to face up to it sometime. Until now I have been sending news back to my family that is optimistic and even cheerful. I do not want to be the bearer of bad news, nor do I want to admit our mistake on such a scale, but I have to be honest. My first letter after arriving in Keith takes over a week to write, but at least by then Eric and I are all the more convinced we have to find a way out of our present situation.

*Keith 20/11/49*

*My dear Elsie and Alan,*

*By the time you receive this I hope you will have read the letter sent to Joan from Adelaide. I asked her to send it on as it contained most of the news from the last night before leaving the ship, and up to now have not had many chances of writing. It was simply lovely to receive your letters. I cannot describe what they mean when one is far away from home for this will never be home for me in spite of Eric and Susan. Even Eric wants to go back and we have tried to get away but it's no use.*

*I don't want you to have a wrong impression of*

*Hurtle and Grace. They are very kind and sincere people and all the people we have met are the same. Eric finds he cannot make headway as a butcher especially as regards killing. Of course I think he will improve as time goes on, but what with the weather, the flies, sanitation etc, he felt he'd made a mistake. They had only just moved into this house, and it's in a very rough state. We are sleeping out at another house.*

*I suppose when Grace and Hurtle get a chance things will be different here, but Hurtle has collapsed twice recently and really should be off work altogether. He wants Eric to take over the books and delivering. For the time being he is paying him £5 per week and our keep, to be adjusted when we go in our own home, so that's very good isn't it? A house is being built by the man who owns the shop, next door to the shop, which we are supposed to be going in. There are two rooms at the back of the shop and as soon as we can fix them up we are going there and I think we will be happier when we can do things our own way.*

*At the moment we don't get any evenings. Tea which is like dinner occurs about 6.30 to 7, then we get the 3 kiddies in bed which is nearly 8 o'clock and then there is the washing up for 7 of us. Every drop of water has to be carried in and boiled on an iron stove which burns wood. No sink, only a bowl & tray on the kitchen table. Then the men are so tired and usually have to be up at 5 or 6 o'clock, so it's off to bed soon after 9pm most nights. I suppose I'm soft but I wouldn't like a life like Grace's. I help her as much as I possibly can – not that she wants me to.*

*Quite apart from the country life, which no doubt is much the same in England, I am not impressed with Australia. The weather is different every day.*

*One day it's cold and windy, the next very hot and sultry. Some days have been lovely, but only a few. Grace says it's terrible during December and January, and a lot of women seem to get up at 5am to do their washing as it's such an exhausting business especially in the heat of the day. Fruit and veg are about the same price as at home.*

*Keith is quite a nice little village but the countryside is quite different to England – sort of scrubby and untidy, but pretty in spots. I think we would like it better in the town suburbs as everything is so different here, but at the moment I am hoping we can get away in a few years time and come home. We should be able to put some money away and up to now Eric has not had asthma, but I really think it's because he has had so much to do and gets really physically tired. Today is Sunday and they are out at the farm killing. Goodness knows when they will be back! Susan seems to be enjoying it but has some real scraps with Geoffrey who is 4 years old.*

*Lots of love to you all, please write as often as you can. Am looking forward to the photos and Mrs Dale's Diary.*

*Mollie*

*PS – We'll have some snaps soon.*

Outside the shop at Keith

"On the wrong side of the tracks." "The poor side of town." They are both expressions that come to mind on the day I go with Grace to look at the butcher's shop – and the site of our future home. But which is the wrong side? Is it where we are living? Or where we are *going* to live?

Grace and Hurtle's house is on the north of the railway line, in one of a few scattered homesteads nearer to land reserved for pasture. The commercial centre of Keith – a scattering of houses, a church, a bank, a post office, a hotel and a few shops are on the south side. The latest addition is about to open as a butcher's, stocked with freshly slaughtered meat from the farm, and it will be *me* who will be serving behind the counter! Just one more instance of a misrepresentation of the Australian Dream.

I find myself thinking back to a conversation with Mrs Solomons in our little cabin aboard *Esperance Bay*. She had lost her husband in the war, and accepted an invitation to join her elder brother who migrated to Perth in 1937. He's a builder, and work is not in short supply.

'Henry has built his own house, and now he is working on an extension, so he will have plenty of room for Rachel and me.'

'Will it be ready when you get there?' I asked.

Mrs Solomons smiled. 'Probably not! Henry is so dreadfully busy. He gets very little help as there are so few men with the right skills. And the Australian Government pay him a lot of money for every house he finishes, so...' She shrugged her shoulders, a frequent habit of hers, but in the confines of our present situation I thought it rather clever.

We were stretched out on the bottom bunks of our tiny cabin, with both girls asleep above us. My companion was half-sitting, propped up on one elbow, with her head brushing the underside of Rachel's mattress. A childish little cough just inches away reminded me that Susan might yet wake up, so I lowered my voice.

'I should have married a builder... Perhaps I could get Eric to re-think this whole idea!'

'You should! Builders are in such short supply. What about this friend of yours? He has accommodation ready for you?'

I nodded. 'So he says. Eric seems very confident about it all. Apparently there are also tax incentives for farmers to produce meat and wool, so Hurtle found it better to grow sheep rather than crops. He's already built his own house, and as he wants Eric to help with the business side, he's bought a shop too and we should be living right next door to it.'

'So you won't be farming yourself, then?'

'No. The way I understand it is Eric will take over the shop side of the business once there's enough income to support both families.'

It all sounded so straightforward and simple then, in relaxed conversation with Mrs Solomons. But now I stand on this dusty backwoods street in the middle of nowhere, and find my confidence wobbling. The building in front of me bears no comparison to my brother-in-law's tidy little butcher's shop in Chorlton.

From the outside I have to admit it shows potential. It stands proudly detached from any other structure on the street, and it is only a few minutes' walk from the bank and the post office. A decorative but functional canopy shelters the double-fronted windows from the invasive rays of the sun. Brick and stone-built, unlike so many of its wooden neighbours, it can remain relatively cool inside on the hottest days, and contains a huge refrigerator in the back (powered by mains electricity). Alongside are two rooms large enough for storage or, with the provision of cooking and washing facilities, temporary accommodation for a small family. I remember my own two-bed house in Chorlton, so much larger by comparison, and try to imagine how I can transform this relatively primitive situation into something like the one I imagined such a short time ago.

The drudgery of domestic life within our new household can improve, of course – but will Eric be able to get away from the slaughtering and butchery that Hurtle has persuaded him to do? Susan is now one of three children living in the same house, two of them under school age, and has never had to cope with other siblings. As her parents we have to consider how practical our current situation might be, whether there really is scope for improvement on our own initiative, or if it will be better to hope for a return ticket.

The post becomes my lifeline. Letters crossing the miles from England are a vital means of support when I feel stuck in the middle of nowhere. Every day without receiving mail makes the chores a heavier burden. I console myself by picturing the next letter from Elsie, Alan, Joan or even Bert. I see it in my mind, sitting in a sack that is even now being unloaded from an aircraft on Australian soil. Such a journey either way could take anything from a week to two weeks before arrival, and I find myself snatching any free moment I can to sit at a table and write. The flow of words between home and our present abode is not as constant as I would like, but it is not for want of trying.

*23rd November 1949 – Keith*

As the weeks pass I assume an even greater role of care. Our isolated situation means I have a deeper responsibility in providing for my daughter and my naive yet hard-working husband. Eric might be earning our keep, but I have to be a source of warmth and comfort to both. We are in a mess of our own making, but I know we can get through it. At least – I hope so.

We lie cuddled together under a sheet and two blankets. Despite the heat of the day the night temperature in our bedroom has dropped to make us feel chilly without the additional layers. Neither of us has found sleep, and both have plenty on our minds. My eyes are open, but it is my thoughts that are focussed.

'Do you still have faith in Hurtle?'

'Yes,' is Eric's eventual response. 'Yes, I think so. He certainly works hard.'

'Grace, too. She never stops.' I stay silent for a moment, trying to find the right words. 'Eric, are we doing the right thing?'

He gives a heavy sigh. This is such a familiar subject of conversation that he can't help himself. Eric has always had such a strong belief in his own actions that I am sure it still shocks him to admit he'd got it wrong this time. Now our very survival as a family is in doubt. Where can we go from here?

'I don't think we have any choice,' he says. 'You saw the letter from the Immigration Office. They can't help us.'

I turn over and push myself up onto my elbow. 'But

there will be a time when we can go home? We can't stay here, Eric. We can't!'

I can make out the shape of his face in the gloom, and I fancy I can even see the pain in my eyes reflected in Eric's. He reaches out and closes his hand over my arm.

'One day. As soon as we can, love. I promise. I'm going to have a word with Hurtle in the morning. He still thinks we're here permanently, so I'm going to have to be straight with him. He has to know.'

But a day later we are no further forward. Eric and Hurtle return from the farm earlier than I expect, and I am sat with Susan and Lorraine in the living room for a few minutes while Grace goes to pick up Geoffrey from school. The temperature has been fairly temperate at around eighty five degrees, but there is only the screen door between me and the boys as I hear them climb out of the cab.

'Stone me, Eric. You've got to look at what's on offer out here! Your own business, for God's sake! I've put a lot of thought into this, and a heap of effort too. Sure you've taken a risk, but so have I... Give it time, that's what I say. Give Mollie more time. She'll get used to it – they all do. Grace'll show her all she needs to know.'

I can see the two men facing each other at the side of the cab, and Eric makes one last plea: 'It's not just Grace and Mollie. It's you and me! I know I'm never going to make it as a butcher...'

'You don't have to. I've seen you. I know you're as bad as a Sheila at the sight of blood!' Hurtle starts up the path. 'C'mon, Eric my old pal, have some trust. You can buy the butcher's business off me when the time's right, and get some boys in to do all the stuff you don't want to do. You're the boss, right? So you just balance the books and pay some other beggar to do the rest. What's wrong with that?'

The screen door is flung wide open and Hurtle stomps inside, glancing at the three of us before heading for the kitchen without even a 'G'day'. Eric follows him in, looking exhausted and shame-faced. Seeing the three of us sat on the floor, he stops abruptly. I suppose he can tell from the look on my face I have heard every word.

Our bedroom hut

*December 1949 – Keith*

As 1949 draws to a close I learn how to run a butcher's shop, surprising myself that I begin to enjoy the responsibility. Some of my customers become "regulars" and I learn so much more about Keith and its community. People here are much the same as those in Manchester in that they like to talk. The chief topic of conversation is the situation in China, where Mao Tse-tung's Communist Party has just taken control, and the world seems to be holding its breath while it awaits the outcome. In England I might not have shown any interest, as it would have seemed too far away. But here we are well aware how highly charged this situation is for such a near neighbour. We have left the frying pan of uncertainty in Europe; could we be facing the fire of similar confusion in the Pacific? On a more light-hearted note, one piece of news I learn on a very hot day is the news that *Baby, it's Cold Outside* is the most popular song of the week. But life in general – like the temperature – is far from comfortable for our little family.

*Friday 16/12/49*

*My dear Elsie and Alan,*

*Thank you so very much for your letters, and I do hope since writing them you have received another one from me. Your birthday letter did come on the DAY, Elsie. I was so glad to have it, that's a lovely little verse which I shall remember. Thank you too for Mrs Dale's Diary. I shall look forward to the next instalment.*

*Today it is so hot we don't know what to do for the coolest. Fortunately Grace has a fridge and is making a cool orange drink. This house is wooden and gets very hot. We have been trying to get the children to lie down but it's too hot even on the beds so now they are lying on the kitchen floor eating ice blocks – I feel like joining them!*

*Actually I should be walking over to the shop to finish off our rooms and buy some cups etc, as we hope to move there this week-end. I shall be glad as the room is stone and will be a bit cooler. The hut for the bedroom is wooden, but then up to now the nights have been quite chilly.*

*Hurtle has borrowed a kerosene stove for us to cook on, until the fireplace is built. It is like a double primus, so it will be quite a job getting enough hot water and cooking meals on it as well. Still it's better than keeping our wood stove going in this weather.*

*Eric is settling down better now and says he can stick it if I can, but I am not prepared to stay here always. We told Hurtle we didn't know if we should be staying permanently. His idea seems to be to get the butchery organised properly and then sell it to Eric. Of course it is an opportunity to make some money I daresay, but to my mind the person that owns the business should be able to do all the work, not just the books.*

*Hurtle is a very decent sort, but the kind that drives himself to the last half ounce. He says he started this butchery for Eric, but Grace says he would have done it in any case as they had to move into Keith for Geoffrey's schooling and Hurtle had to do something here. I think Eric is going to see how the first 12 months goes.*

*Susan puts you both in her prayers and says she wants to go and see you and Auntie Elsie to dress her. She has got terribly rough and naughty since she mixed with other children, especially Geoffrey. There is a lot of polio about – 450 cases in Adelaide. Healthy my eye! I was hoping to send some snaps but they are not quite ready, with an enlargement.*

*I shall be thinking of you all on Christmas Day – very specially. How I do hope it won't be too many years before we are together again.*

*Lots and lots of love to both and Joan too, as she may be with you when this letter arrives.*

*Very Merry Xmas.*

*Mollie*

Left to Right: Susan, Mollie, Grace, Hurtle, Geoffrey and Lorraine

*25th December 1949 – Keith*

We spend Christmas Day at Hurtle's house. It is not where I want to be. Children's voices fill the air in play, but I brace myself for the inevitable scream of frustration from one little girl. It is an emotion I can relate to, but for me, screaming is against the rules.

In consolation I find myself some space and unfold a

precious sheet of blue paper which bears my sister's handwriting. I have read it over so many times I can quote from it verbatim, and I know I will cry again as I read it once more, but I can't help myself. The words on the page are a potent addiction.

'What are you doing?'

Eric has found me out. I quickly re-fold the paper and wipe a partially formed tear from the corner of my eye, then turn to face him with a ready smile.

'Oh, just reading Joan's letter again. Who would have thought letters could mean so much? Her's and Elsie's – especially on Christmas Day.'

Eric gives me a broad smile of understanding. I've never been able to resist the effect this has on me. His is such a gentle face, now deeply tanned, but with lines that seem deeper etched at the corner of his mouth than a year ago. He has his shirt sleeves rolled up above his elbows, and is wearing clean work trousers although today is officially his first day off in over a month. By contrast I am still pale-skinned and wearing a cotton print frock with short sleeves. We are in Grace's kitchen – the coolest place indoors on Christmas Day, while the presently playful screams and shouts of three young children float in through the open door on the hot dry air of the Australian summer. I lean over the work-table and peer out through the window.

'She loves that pram. And it's bigger and better than Lorraine's.'

Eric joins me at the window. 'It had to be bigger. Look how tiny Lorraine is!'

For a moment we stand in silence, watching our daughter racing a shiny pink toy pram around a tree in hot pursuit of a red pedal car. Four year old Geoffrey is the driver, and his small dungaree-clad frame is leaning forward, hunched over the steering wheel while shouting insults over his shoulder at his younger sister. The little girl is oblivious to his cries, constantly blowing raspberries while pushing her own tiny pram in the opposite direction. A cheery adult laugh bursts from somewhere outside our viewpoint, reminding us that Hurtle is still sat in the shade of the house, where he and Grace are "officially" acting as race referees.

'Merry Christmas, love!' I am aware of the emotion in my own voice as Eric turns his head to look at me.

'Doesn't seem right, does it?' he acknowledges. I watch the reaction in his eyes. 'I mean with the heat and the sun, and all this... Not like last year.'

I swallow and turn back to the window. I have been trying not to think back to that time. 'You're tired, aren't you? You must be exhausted, working all those hours every day. Hurtle's used to it and I know he's been far from well since we got here.'

Eric glances at the open doorway. Then he takes my hand and steers me gently through to the living room, signalling me to be quiet by placing his finger to his lips.

'What?' I whisper.

'That's the point. Hurtle's selling up.'

'What?! What do you mean?' I struggle to keep my voice low, immediately conscious of the importance of this news. My excitement only grows as he explains about his recent conversation with Hurtle.

'He really needs four men on a full time basis, and there's just no one out there. He knows how I feel, and that I'm not suited to this kind of life. Same for you. To be honest I think he sees you as the major obstacle... No, no – let me finish. I've told him straight it's not just you. I've got to look at the whole picture. Anyway, to cut the story short, Hurtle has made a decision. He's selling the farm, the shop and this place, and he says he's going to take a break. So – we should be packing up again before long.'

Female laughter and footsteps on the stone kitchen floor cut the conversation short, and Grace is calling us back outside. But as we return into the blazing sunshine to retrieve Susan from a confrontation with Geoffrey, I feel my heart racing at the glimpse of hope that has just been offered. I even smile at Hurtle as I consider if my husband has just given me the best Christmas present I can remember.

*Dec 28th/49*

*My dear Elsie and Alan,*

*Thank you so very much Elsie for your Xmas letter which arrived just when we needed it most – on the 24th. There was one from Joan too, we sat and read them and thought about you all at home. I'm very glad the tea arrived safely, but it's funny about the letters. I'm sure I have written several since we arrived and hope this one reaches you safely.*

*According to the paper you have had a mild Christmas. Here it has been very hot and then most nights it suddenly goes quite cold. We spent Xmas Day with Hurtle and his family. They were very kind but it was so hot in their wooden house. We had plenty to eat of course, but the happiest part of the day was Susan's little face when she saw the pram Father Christmas had brought.*

*There is a little kitten here at the shop. You can imagine what a life it has and how the poor thing gets pushed around in the pram. On Xmas Eve there was a little open air party for all the children in a field nearby. They all had gifts, ice cream and cool drinks, to which Susan did great justice. She received a large duck and was very thrilled. She never forgets you and when I was going through the photos the other day said she wanted to go and see you and Auntie Joan.*

*I don't know whether I hardly dare write it, but*

*(hush, it seems too good to be true) we may be coming home!! Hurtle has decided to sell everything up including the farm and take a holiday. He wants to keep Eric though he knows we are not very keen. He thinks I'm the stumbling block but a fortnight ago I had agreed with Eric to try and stick it for a few years. We moved into this room behind the shop and I ordered things we will need. However, if Eric doesn't want to stay I shall be only too happy to come home, though I think this really is a land of opportunity if you can rough it and work very, very hard.*

*Thursday morning*
*Please don't take too much notice of what I said about coming home. Hurtle has been talking to Eric and I am not going to influence him for coming home, though I want to desperately.*

*It is another very hot sticky day, and I cannot walk out in the sun. This room is cooler than Hurtle's home, because the walls are stone, the roof corrugated iron. It looks awful just now as the floor is bare, the walls peeling, full of holes and cracks. I ordered a congoleum square which hasn't come yet. Some day a wood stove is to be built in this room so it's no use bothering about the walls, but of course we shall be leaving here when the business is sold. I wonder just what will happen, and where next.*

*Will you be going to the Watch Night Service I wonder? Lots of luck for the New Year and lots of love.*

*Mollie*

*PS – Thanks very much for that lovely card and photo. I'd love to know what Alan was saying. M.*

Our "Merry" Christmas is shortly followed by wishes for a "Happy" New Year. As the midnight hour grows closer, together with the start of a new decade, I cannot help but contemplate what my future might be. In the last five years I have lost both parents, got married and had a child – and moved as far away from the rest of my family as it is possible to go. Where will we be in another five years? The newspapers tell us that, on top of the situation in China, President Truman in the USA is warning about the nuclear capabilities of the Soviets. They say a Cold War is coming. I feel locked into something similar, so I know what that feels like. Of course it is true I love my daughter and my husband, but I do not love what we are doing with our lives. We are trying to live as Australians, but my English heart isn't beating to the same rhythm.

Hurtle has made the decision to sell, but that simply leaves Eric and I in a very uncertain place. While he favours looking at options that might help us settle somewhere in Australia, I prefer to book a return voyage – assuming we can afford it. But Eric argues we have come so far, what is the point in giving up at the first hurdle? My communications with "home" are a major comfort, each letter arriving from England as addictive as oxygen. I revel in every titbit of news about family and friends, of our church and my parents' grave, and even about the forthcoming General Election.

With the New Year only one week old, it is Eric who first puts pen to paper.

*Keith, S. Australia*
*8th January 1950*

*My dear Elsie and Alan,*

*When you've recovered from your shock to find I*

*am still alive (tho' it's a wonder I am) I would first of all like to thank you for the book, which arrived in the parcel last Friday. I was simply hungry for something to read, and devoured it straight away. It was a good book. Fortunately, I've had a free weekend this week except for doing the books and I lay on the bed (we've no easy chairs now) and read it in between dozing or catching up on my sleep.*

*This is the first free weekend I've had since I came here. Last week was a holiday but even then we had to work, but I think Hurtle is afraid I'll crack up soon. So he went out to the farm and did the killing himself today, taking Ken Mitchell, who is one of his neighbours, to help with the slaughtering. Well, I'll never make a butcher. I just can't kill a sheep like they do, and they think nothing of it. I can't skin one either, although I've tried. I'm sick and tired of cleaning up, which is all left to me, and making sausages. I don't mind wrapping the orders up and keeping the books, but I was never cut out for this kind of work as I begin to realise now.*

*We've got far too much for just two of us and are at work from 6 o'clock in the morning often till 9 or 10, 11 or 12 at night. In fact I'm so busy I don't have time to worry if I've got asthma or not. As a matter of fact I've had no attacks while I've been here, and have taken no tablets whatsoever, but it's a comfortless life.*

*We live in one room behind this shop and sleep in a wooden hut in what is called a garden I suppose. Really it is like camping out. We have a primus stove to cook on, and you should see our bathroom. It is the latest thing in corrugated iron, probably erected during the first year of this century. It has no door and is just a lean-to adjoining our kitchen. We do have a bath however, and use it once a week, heating the water in a large wood fire copper and carrying it by bucket to the bath. Susan has her bath first, then while Daddy puts her to bed Mummy adds a little more hot water and gets in herself. When she has finished and the water is just like mud, Daddy has to jump in and tub himself. Susan has one inch of water, Mummy an inch and a half, and Daddy has another half inch (chiefly mud).*

*Of course it's nice and draughty, and it's cold in the summer at present, so goodness knows what it will be like in the winter. I'm afraid we won't be here then however, but will most likely be on our way back to England, Home and Beauty.*

*We went for a walk this morning. Of course everyone must have thought us mad. But as only mad dogs and Englishmen go out in the mid-day sun – we went. We went up the road to the slaughter house (the local one, not the one at the farm) and I showed Mollie where we did the killing, and then we went down another road back home. When we got there we both had halo's. I had a big one because I had Susan on my shoulders – a halo of flies.*

*Flies, flies – talking of flies the whole country wants soaking in DDT. I've never seen so many, and I've been places. First of all and worst of all are the blowflies. Then there's the small housefly, and maggots breed everywhere. We have a fearful job trying to keep the flies off the meat. Some days however there aren't many about and other days there are millions of 'em. Fortunately there are no mosquitoes here.*

*If you can imagine miles and miles of absolutely nothing but flat land with quite a lot of gum trees, and buildings scattered all over the place, you'll have some idea of Keith. I will draw a little diagram of the layout of the village, which is somewhat out of proportion, but the map I've drawn is about a quarter mile square.*

*Eric*

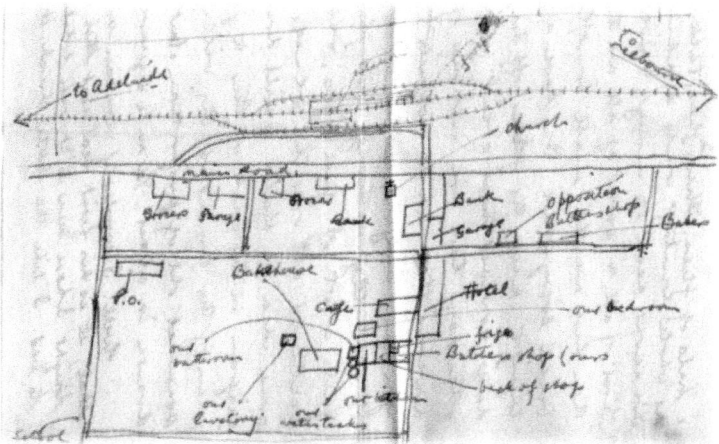

*Well! I wonder if you can understand all that. It is his first real rest this week-end, and tonight I have been to Church whilst he put Susan to bed. I like the little church, it is Congregational and they have exactly the same hymn books as Zion so I felt at home.*

*Thank you so very much for those lovely presents. Never before have I owned such a beautiful brush and comb, but I am putting it away and not using it in this dirty place. As for Susan, you should have seen her face! I think she just couldn't believe the bag was really hers. She has wanted one since Christmas when Lorraine had one given her. She was very pleased too to have June's bonnet and the iron. She often talks of you both and says* "We shall have to go and see them won't we Mum, on a big ship." *I am hoping so much that it might come true but daren't set up too many hopes.*

*Eric has gone off to bed in our little wooden hut*

*and I must go too. It seems creepy here with the sound of the fridge going, and we have to be up early, so Goodnight and God bless you both always.*
*Very much love*

*Mollie, Eric and Susan*

*11ᵗʰ January 1950 – Keith*

The Australian summer temperature is as relentless as the flies competing for space on the meat carcasses. But knowing his days of butchering sheep are numbered, Eric seems to accept the opportunity for any other kind of life in Australia is simply not on offer. He has switched his attention to the practicalities of arranging a passage home. In my heart I still feel optimistic he will find a way, but my head tells me to remain realistic and accept whatever fate I might meet as a pommie's wife. So I do my duty and man the counter in the shop.

The heat this January is enough to melt the glass in the window – or at least, that is how it seems to me. Despite the shade from a huge canopy straddling the front of the premises, the joints in the wooden door have swollen and become distorted without any layer of protective paint. It is always a battle to pull the door closed (and then open it again) if the shop has to be locked for any reason during the middle part of the day. This is my present dilemma.

I was fairly busy for an hour or so, handing out regular customer orders to several ladies calling to collect before the sun is at its highest. Sausages, chops, shoulders and even whole sheep legs have been pulled out of the huge refrigerator at the back of the shop, marked off the day's tally, and carried away after some brief but friendly conversations. Then Gladys calls for her daily stash (as she calls the five and a half pounds of mince that is central to her normal routine). Hurtle's younger sister likes to talk, and to this English girl in particular. In cooler climates there might be more appeal to such pleasantries for me, but the incessant heat and the battles with the flies are undesirable distractions.

We've been talking for around ten minutes when a welcome diversion intervenes. A distant throbbing from the motor of a heavy wagon heralds the arrival of the vehicle itself, instantly eclipsing the sunshine that has baked the street outside all morning; and the curtained gloom that results inside the shop makes even Gladys pause for breath.

'So he's not had his asthma at all? That's good. Oh, what's this then? Are you expecting something, dear? He's stopped right outside.'

'Why no, I don't think... Oh!' I pause as my brain makes a tentative connection. 'I wonder if...'

But just then the fly-screen door to the shop is pulled open by a big bear of a man, pot-belly prominent behind a sweat-stained brown shirt, topped with a grubby apron of bleached leather.

'Weal? I'm looking for a Weal?'

I can barely conceal my amusement as I correct the man. 'I think you'll find it's *Veale* – but yes, you're in the right place. Can you bring it round the back, please? Sorry Gladys, but I've been waiting for this for weeks.'

'Ooh! Is it your sideboard? Good on yer, girl. It's about bloody time. How long's it been then?'

I hurry to quash any further attempt at conversation, anxious to put the remaining tray of chops back into the refrigerator and to usher Gladys out of the shop. In the meantime the delivery man has rejoined the driver outside, opening the back of the vehicle so the contents can be inspected and removed.

Now I have to close the shop door to any further customers while I supervise the delivery – and ensure my daughter doesn't get in anyone's way.

'Susan! What are you doing?'

I put all my weight against the door to encourage it to close while calling over my shoulder towards the room at the back of the shop. Through the glass I can see a familiar wooden tea chest being passed out of the wagon into the easy embrace of the shirt-sleeved delivery man.

'I'm shopping.'

The explanation comes from the doorway behind me, where Susan is stood with her small feet thrust into a pair of my shoes. She is also carrying a little pink leather handbag that is a prized Christmas present from her auntie.

'Oh, this blessed door! Susan dear – put my shoes away, please, and put the bag down. You'll need to open the screen door and make sure there's space for some men to bring some things in. Hurry, please. We've got some un-packing to do!'

My little helper obediently turns to shuffle her feet into the back room as I give one final heave at the shop door and turn the lock. Through the glass I see the delivery man approaching with the tea chest, so I wave him round to the side of the building before following in my daughter's wake to the Veale family living quarters.

Some fifteen minutes later, the little room behind the butcher's shop has been transformed. Two large tea chests sit in the middle of the floor, occupying the place where a table and three chairs once stood. These we have pushed to one side, together with Susan's drawing materials, while in pride of place along the opposite wall is Mother's magnificent oak sideboard.

We stand looking at it in silence. The two men have made light work of carrying my precious piece of furniture out of their wagon and through the side door. It is pure luck it was the right way round for them to drop gently into the space I had cleared in the few minutes it took to offload.

'Why is that here, Mummy?'

'Because it was Mother's.' But then I realise my

daughter needs a proper response. I kneel down and pull her into my arms.

'You know how you have things that are special to you? Like teddy? Well, this sideboard is special to me because it used to belong to my mummy and daddy, and it was always there when I was a little girl. I remember how my mummy was always polishing it, because she was so proud of it – and now she's not here anymore, I want to look after it for her. So, are you going to help me?'

Susan nods slowly. 'We can polish it every day, can't we? Until your mummy comes back for it.'

I force a smile, understanding the logic of her three year old brain. 'Yes, darling. We'll polish it every day. But we won't unpack everything yet, because we might still have to move somewhere else. Oh! But there's something in one of these that is *very* important.'

I turn to inspect the two chests. Checking the labels and the markings on the sides, I select one and pull the top open. Inside are some wads of screwed-up newspaper (*English* newspaper!) together with a bag of material. But then I plunge my hand deeper inside and heave out a heavy wooden box with a curved top to its dark brown casing. There is a single word etched in gold leaf on the side which gives a clue to its contents: *Singer*. I clear a space before setting it down on the table.

'Ah-ha! Here we are. Now I can get busy! What has Mummy been saying I would do for you soon?'

Susan pulls a face. 'Find my bucket and spade?'

I laugh. 'No, silly! This is my sewing machine. So now I can start to make you some more frocks. Look at you – the ones you have now are getting far too small. So Mummy has to get busy and make some more.'

But I will have no further time to spare on domestic matters. A heavy knocking from nearby announces the arrival of another customer, and I hurry through to open the door. It stays firmly closed, denying any attempt I make to force it ajar before I recognise where the problem lies.

'Susan! What have you done with the keys?'

I turn to find the suspect just behind me, clutching a pink leather object to her chest.

'I might have known...' I shake my head in mock exasperation and hold my hand out for the little handbag.


Some days are worse for me because of their emotional attachment. December has been difficult because I had my own birthday on the fourteenth, and then Christmas of course just two weeks later. Previously those occasions have been happy family events, shared with the people I have been close to all my life, as well as with Eric and Susan. It is so easy to think back to days full of laughter and warm hugs, parlour games and toasts to our future. Even the War never took those days away from us. But now I feel so dreadfully alone and unsure of the future, and January brings two more birthdays: Joan's and then Alan's. I feel like a naughty little girl who has not been invited to a party, and it hurts.


*Saturday 28/1/50*
*8.30 p.m.*

*My dear Elsie and Alan,*

*Eric is out slaughtering with Hurtle and I am getting his tea ready on our little primus. It's quite a problem, which shall I do first, boil the kettle as he will want a drink, or do the chips, and then he might like some steak cooking (that may make your mouth water I suppose, but I'm tired of the sight of it and long for a bit of fish!). I have just bathed Susan and am longing to go and get in myself, but our bathroom has no door on it and people keep calling for meat orders, so shall have to wait until Eric comes home. It's been very hot again and it's no cooler tonight, feels like a thunderstorm brewing. Elsie, please forgive me about the mop bucket, I remember you asking me and thought I had replied but must blame it on the heat. It seems to paralyse my brain as well as my body, especially when writing letters.*

*It was so good of you to mention sending the spare part, but I don't think I'll bother now as I'm hoping we may not be stopping here. Last Sunday Eric wrote the Immigration people as to how we could return to England, and today we have had a reply. It's rather vague but we gather from it that it would be a free passage.*

*Sunday*
*They say "You are under no financial obligation to remain in Australia". You know I cannot realise that my nightmare of the past 16 months might really end, and yet at the same time I am sorry that things have been so very disappointing for Eric. We cannot really blame Hurtle as other people have let him down and the business has become too large for him to handle, but I do think he was wrong to be in such a hurry to get us out here when there was no real accommodation. He cannot understand why we want to go back, but we cannot see any possibility of a decent job or a home of our own. There are plenty of jobs advertised in the paper in Adelaide, but no accommodation. In any case, I think the Australian summers are lousy and Eric agrees with me. Today is just as bad as yesterday only clammier!*

*Anyway that's enough grousing. You'll think I can do nothing else, but we do have a good laugh over our troubles. After all it's our own fault. Susan gave us a good laugh yesterday, I found she had emptied half a bottle of liquid shampoo over Hurtle's dog. She said she was washing it – it smelt like a chemist's shop. By the way she wants a letter "all of her own" so will you send her one?*

*Thanks for Mrs Dale's Diary – poor woman. What complications!*

*Our love to you both always.*

*Mollie, Eric and Susan*

*PS – If we should come home this summer, do you think you could put up with us for a short while? M.*

Keith Congregational Church c 1910

*5ᵗʰ February 1950 – Keith*

There are only fifteen members in the congregation this morning, but the minister seems pleased with the turnout in the tiny church. It has been good for all of us to share some strength behind the vocals of the last hymn *All Things Bright and Beautiful* (a personal favourite of mine), even if our daughter's contribution has been more enthusiastic than tuneful.

'Mr and Mrs Veale, I think I heard a promising soprano there!'

The Reverend George Alcock is taking his customary farewells by the porch, and we are the last to exit. A round-faced man with thinning gingery hair, he smiles at Susan in her newly made cotton frock – but her frowning reaction is not encouraging.

'One of her better days!' her father quips. 'You should hear her in the bath. In fact, you probably have!'

We all laugh, but our little imp remains solemn-faced, vigorously swinging her little handbag in her free hand. I feel I have to offer an explanation.

'Susan didn't want to come today, Mr Alcock. She's got a big drawing project on the go, and she wanted Daddy to make her an easel this morning.'

'I DID want to come! I just want Daddy to help me NOW!'

Worn down by female attrition, Eric reaches down to lift her onto his hip. 'It's okay Sue! We're going to get busy any minute now. We just have to say goodbye properly, that's all.'

The minister takes my proffered hand briefly after giving my husband a firm handshake. 'Goodbye Eric. Lovely to see the whole family. Mrs Veale, could I ask you to stay for a moment? I promise I won't keep you any longer than I have to.'

Eric smiles, obviously pleased the minister has remembered his Christian name. He gives him the same courtesy.

'Bye George. I'll see you next week. Come on Suey. Let's go and sort out that artist studio of ours.'

I am sitting in the minister's vestry, a room hardly bigger than a cupboard at the back of the building. Its principal function seems to be for a change of clothing and to provide a table and chair for making notes. George Alcock goes to retrieve a second chair from the church hall, while I wait and wonder what the minister's interest might be. Has Susan's loud and animated singing brought a genuine complaint? But the man is smiling as he returns to sit opposite me.

'I'm sorry to sound so formal, calling you "Mrs Veale", but I'm not sure how to address you. You appear to have two Christian names?'

I laugh, a little embarrassed. 'Yes – my birth name is Mary, but everyone calls me Mollie. It's how I prefer it.'

'I see. Well, Mollie – I should like you to call me George, and I've a favour to ask you. We're only a very small community in Keith, as you know, so I often have to ask favours!'

He pauses, but I'm not sure how I should react, so I just nod.

'It's the Harvest Festival in a few weeks time, and I know Hurtle has promised a generous donation, as has his... er – competitor in town. We are obviously hoping for all manner of pastoral contributions to make a decent display in church, and of course to pass on to the more needy members of this parish. But what I really would like to do this year is to encourage other community members to come along and join in. So I'm planning a special service that includes a choir.'

We stare at each other for a moment. I'm still not sure what kind of favour George is after, but I smile in response.

'That sounds lovely!'

I wonder if he wants a financial contribution. He's going to be unlucky if that is the case...

'So you'll be happy to join us?'

Eric is pleased with his efforts at constructing a miniature artist's easel. It is functional if not aesthetically pleasing on the eye – made from discarded pieces of timber he found in one of Hurtle's outhouses. They have all been cleaned properly the previous day, and it has only taken twenty minutes to put together in our multi-purpose room at the back of the shop. A sheet of paper has been tacked to the board, and now we stand watching as our three-and-three-quarter-year-old artist works on her own interpretation of her father's construction work that morning.

'You? You're going to sing in a choir?'

I grin proudly. 'Yes, I am! It's only for this one occasion, of course. But it was nice to be asked, so I said yes. He does know we're not going to be here indefinitely.'

'Jungle drums. I don't expect anything stays secret for long in a place this size. I suppose Hurtle or Grace will have said something.'

'Grace told him about selling the farm, yes. We had a nice little chat, actually. I told George about you writing to the Immigration people. He said it's quite a common thing with Brits. Lots settle in the cities where there's a better chance of getting paid a decent wage. But most have to rent a room somewhere because of the price of houses. A minister and his wife he knows came over from England a few years ago, and they eventually rented from a Housing Trust – but they had to wait six months before they even got on the waiting list. Another couple he knows just bought a house and it cost them over two thousand pounds!'

'*Two* thousand? Ha! That's ridiculous. We'd pay at least half that in England.' Eric hands me a glass of water he had been chilling in a jug in the fridge since he returned from church. The day seems to be getting even hotter, and I feel my blouse prickling around my waistband as I gulp down the precious liquid.

'We'd never be able to save that kind of money. Hey look! Not a bad resemblance!'

I put the glass down and look closer at my daughter's efforts with a brown pencil.

'Oh, that's lovely darling. But why on earth have you given Daddy a halo?'

*Saturday Feb 11th/50.*

*My dear Elsie and Alan,*

*Thank you very much Elsie for letter no. 2. Yes, we have been sizzling again but only a few days this time. It's been lovely today and quite chilly tonight.*

*We haven't heard anything definite from the Immigration yet, but our letter asking them to arrange a passage home would only reach them last Tuesday. I expect there will be some objections, but apart from the fact that we both want to leave there is nothing else we can do, other than living in rooms with no possibility of a home of our own for years. There are plenty of jobs in Adelaide, but very few rooms to let, and houses for sale are very limited at terrific prices.*

*Hurtle asked Eric today if we could go to the Immigration Hostel in Adelaide, should he sell the business quickly. Apparently there is somebody interested. Of course he thinks we ought to stay here, but I'm afraid we are not tough enough. Eric could probably manage on his own, but we don't want to live in rooms for goodness knows how many years trying to bring up a family. How are house prices now in England? We shall have to begin again. Of course, I still feel that we shall have to be right on the ship before I can believe we are coming home.*

*Susan received the "Babes in the Wood" book on Thursday. You should have seen her face – a letter of her own! And then immediately out came the coloured pencils. It's a lovely little book.*

*I was practising with the church choir the other day. Yes, fancy roping <u>me</u> in to sing. It reminded me of the war years at Zion when Nancy and I went in the choir. This is just for the Harvest Festival to help out the anthem "Lift up your Heads". There is no proper choir you see as the congregation is very small. People are so scattered, but I think everybody makes an effort for the Harvest. It means so much to them all here.*

*We are going out to a farm tomorrow about 10 miles away. It will be a lovely change for me as I have only been out one car ride since we came. That of course is the only way of getting out apart from a few trains. I have never seen Hurtle's farm.*

*What lots we will have to tell you and you to tell us. Can it really be true we are coming? I do hope and pray we are doing the right thing. Some friends we made on the ship are going to return home and they have a house to themselves, at Lismore on the Queensland border.*

*God bless you both and much love,*

*Mollie*

It is just after ten at night. My letter to Elsie and Alan is written and ready for Eric to post tomorrow. He and Susan are fast asleep in our bedroom hut, and I can hear one of them snoring even above the noise from the fridge on the other side of the wall. As I sit here at the table I find my eyes drawn to Mother's sideboard on my right. It stands there, gleaming proudly against the rough brick wall, totally out of place in this apology for a living-room-come-kitchen. But that only reflects how I feel, a displaced English girl who has somehow lost her way far from home.

I close my eyes, allowing myself to slip back in time to one of the last pleasant memories I have of my time with Mother. I can picture the door at the top of the stairs on that September day in 1946. I hear the muffled response within, and turn the handle before stooping to pick up a tray with the bowl of chicken broth I had made. It was good to see her already sitting up in bed, while still looking frail from influenza.

'That's wonderful, Mollie. Thank you. Sit down, love. I want to talk to you.'

Her request caught me by surprise, as she hadn't been inclined to conversation during her confinement, now stretching into a third week. I sat on the bed and waited while she took a hesitant sip of the hot liquid. We were the same build, slim and small-boned, but to me my mother looked to have become even thinner over the last few months. I watched as she stirred the broth with her spoon before looking up. Lethargic brown eyes peered at me from delicate skin dusted with powder to hide hollow shadows.

'Was that Eric going out?'

'About half an hour ago? Yes, he's gone to spend a few hours with Harold at the shop today.'

'Why?'

'Well, Rita suggested it. She said Harold could do with

some help cutting up the meat each day, and it wouldn't do Eric any harm to learn a trade.'

Mother put down her spoon again after a couple more sips.

'A little too hot, dear. That's good news then. A man needs to feel in control of his life. Perhaps he'll take after his father, then.' She nodded slow approval at her own observation, then looked at me with a tired smile. 'You take after me, don't you?'

'Why do you say that?'

'Because you want things to be right for your husband even more than he does.'

I felt tears welling up behind my eyes. I missed my father so much, and I couldn't begin to think how much worse it must have been for my mother. Her eyes looked paler than they once were, but they still warmed my heart as she continued.

'You've not been married long. What is it – two years? And here you are, squashed up with me. I know it's still been only a year for Eric, not being demobbed straight away, but still... You need to plan for your future. You need to listen to him, Mollie. A wife has to support her husband. That's how life should be.'

I agreed with her, and we let the broth grow cold that afternoon while my baby slept in peace for all of three hours. I told her about Hurtle, and Eric's growing obsession with the idea of moving to Australia. And then Mother simply smiled and patted my arm as she always did. All seemed well with the world. Five months later, she was dead.

There are less than two weeks to go to that dreaded anniversary, and Mother is in my thoughts all the more. Every time I look at her sideboard now I find myself suffering at the pain of my loss while thrilling to the joy of that maternal connection. I remember how her precious antique took pride of place in the dining room at Knutsford

Avenue, and I picture the candlesticks, the fruit bowl and my father's portrait that always adorned it when I was younger. None of those items are there now. I have to protect the surface from the dirt that seems to hang above it in the air. Our wedding photograph already appears to be stained behind the glass, and I am constantly wiping it clean. How could I ever have imagined Australia would be some sort of Paradise?

## *22ⁿᵈ February 1950 – Keith*

I have never been in a car quite like it. The minister offered to take me and Susan out with him when he next went to Bordertown, half an hour's drive away. It would be a special treat, so I picked out my best frock with the silk trim around the neckline, and made sure Susan had a pink ribbon in her hair to complement her own choice of pink and grey cotton print. Now we wait outside the shop front in what little shade the veranda offers at that time of the morning. Promptly at seven o'clock we see a brightly polished vehicle turn the corner by the railway station and head towards us. It looks to me like something the King would drive, and is Henry Ford black, with large chrome and glass headlights perched high above a broad fender. I can clearly see George Alcock and his wife through the windscreen, but which of them is driving?

Australian rules are the same as Britain in that drivers use the left side of the road, and sit on the right hand side of the vehicle. But once the vehicle pulls to a stop opposite, the minister climbs out from behind the steering wheel on the *left* hand side. His wife nods and smiles through the window nearest to us.

'Morning!' the minister calls out. 'I hope we haven't

kept you waiting?'

'Not at all, George. You're right on time. What a lovely car!'

The road is empty of any other traffic, and we cross over to where the minister is holding the rear door open for us with old-world courtesy. The interior is smooth brown leather, and has a warm welcoming odour that instantly brings memories of my father. He spent many years travelling the north-west of England as a commercial salesman. The company he represented manufactured shirts of every kind, but I especially remember the soft leather gloves Father usually wore because of their unique smell. I could see him then, smiling broadly while I sat on his knee at the age of twelve, pulling on his pair of tan gloves with their exquisite stitching. I remember holding the over-sized items to my nose and breathing in their scent, while Father then did the same to my hair. It was a precious memory.

Susan and I are each clutching shopping bags, although the contents are distinctly different: a purse, a string bag and two handkerchiefs in one, a colouring book and pencils in the other.

'Hello Marjorie! It's very kind of you to let us come with you. This is a lovely car.'

The minister's wife smiles as her husband shuts the rear door firmly and then climbs back into his own seat in front of me.

'Hey, we're happy to have the company. And don't start George off about cars. They're a hobby from way back. He'll bore you to death if you let him!'

'Now, now!' says her husband. 'It's a pity Eric couldn't have joined us, Mollie. It would have been a squeeze, mind.'

'Oh, he'd have loved it. But there's no way Hurtle could let him go. They are still so busy out at the farm.'

'I'll bet.'

It is a relatively smooth ride once we re-join the main

highway off the dusty streets of the village, and head out into the flat bush with Mount Monster looming in the near distance to our right. Susan is content to leave her colouring pencils in her basket for once, and sits on my knee, staring out of the window.

'What kind of car is this?'

'Chevrolet. It's American, which is why I'm sitting on this side of the car, in case you were wondering?'

I laugh. 'Yes, I was. When I saw you coming down the road I thought it was Marjorie who was driving!'

'No chance! You'd never get me behind a wheel.'

'I'd never let you,' says George. 'This is a 1934 Master Sedan, and I did it up myself three years ago after rescuing it from a scrap yard in Naracoorte.'

'He won't tell me how much he bought it for, but we had to go on half rations for six months!'

George smiles. 'Not entirely true, but it was worth it. Six cylinders, you know? It can produce up to sixty horsepower when pushed, which isn't bad. More like eighty when new.'

'Oh, change the subject, please!' Marjorie pleads. 'Hey Mollie, I hear your hubby can do a pretty good impression of Stanley Holloway? Is that right?'

'Well, he thinks he can. At least he's pretty good with the monologues. *Albert and the Lion, Sam Small* and all those, you know? Why do you ask?'

'I just love Stanley Holloway! He did a tour over here last year and I'd have loved to go see him, but it's a weekend out to Melbourne and we just couldn't do it. Heard him on the radio though. He's a scream. So we want a private audience with your Eric before you leave town. Does he do requests?'

*Thursday Feb 23rd*

*My dear Elsie and Alan,*

*I am only attempting to write as it is so hot my fingers are sticking to the paper all the time. It is very heavy and grey skies so do hope it will rain soon and put us out of our misery.*

*Susan was very thrilled with your letter Elsie, and listened very solemnly whilst I read it. Yes, she says she does remember Thelma.*

*We have not heard any more from the Immigration people as yet. It seems funny to be waiting again just the same as last year, but with what a difference! They have not raised any objections yet so we take it they are arranging a passage. The butchery is being sold, negotiations are in progress and may be finalised next week, so we may have to go from here quickly. Please keep on writing here until you hear differently.*

*Your Election Day should be just beginning. How I wish we were there. Much interest is being shown here too, and they say we should hear the result by noon on Friday.*

*Tomorrow we are actually having the wood stove put in the kitchen. Of course they would now we shall probably soon be gone. It will be a lovely mess having the wall pulled down. I hope it goes cooler next week and then I can have a baking day!*

*Susan and I had a ride out yesterday. The Minister and his wife were going to Bordertown 28 miles off and suggested we went. It was very hot and couldn't walk about much but we both enjoyed it. Susan quite likes looking in shop windows (there are just a few more than Keith) though of course she keeps spotting things she would like to possess, and we compromise by agreeing she will have them one day* "when Mummy has a lot of pennies"!!!?

*We missed seeing a big snake in the village not long ago, and last week Eric saw a fairly big one near the slaughter yard.*

*Elsie, if you hear anyone grumbling in the greengrocers, tell them I have just had to pay 2/2d for a cabbage, and 2/6d for 6 oranges, ordinary size ones. Plums have never been less than 10d a pound, and carrots 9d with all the green tops on. I thought I should be able to give Susan lots of orange juice made with the real thing.*

*Tomorrow I am taking a small part in the Service for the Women's Day of Prayer. Gosh, I hope it is not so hot and humid.*

*We are looking forward to Alan's letter, and hope you are both well and your mother and sisters alright, Elsie. Do give them our love, and lots of love to both of you from*

*Mollie.*

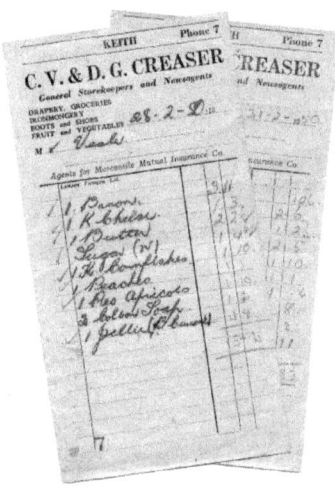

*7ᵗʰ March 1950 – Keith*

While we savour the personal news from every letter we receive with huge satisfaction, I also enjoy poring over newspapers for every titbit of information about life back in Britain. I read that Election Day saw the Labour Party retain a slim lead in the polls over the Conservatives, so there will be no change of government. That must have been a big disappointment for many, as we'd been certain Winston would soon be back in Number 10. Clement Attlee's party had stormed to power at the end of the War with a majority of a hundred and forty six. Now that has been reduced to just fifteen, barely holding Churchill's opposition at bay.

It may have been the uncertainty of the British economy that influenced my brother and sister-in-law to consider moving home, potentially downsizing to something that suits a couple with no children of their own. This is one piece of news that comes in a letter at the beginning of March. Alan felt it only fair to warn us of this possible change because, if the Veale's were to obtain a passage back to England, we would need another temporary roof over our heads. Younger brother Bert's house is smaller, and they have a baby to look after. Joan is still in London, so Eric might have to make enquiries of his own father, currently living near Stockport. I am hoping it won't come to that, as father and son mix about as well as oil and water.

'Well, now we know!'

I look up from our dining table as Eric comes through the door. I have just started a reply to Elsie and Alan, and hope he will have more news. He has been over to Hurtle's house to ask if they have received any more post for us. Every day we expect to hear from the Immigration people, and they always write to us via Hurtle's home address.

'What did they say?'

Eric shakes his head and sits down on the other side of the table. 'Not them. Hurtle. He's finally got round to details.'

'Oh!' I put my pen aside and look up expectantly. 'So where are we going?'

'Would you believe – Delamere?' Eric's face is creased in a broad smile as he sees my reaction. 'No, don't get excited. I don't mean Delamere Forest in Cheshire. It's a little place by the coast somewhere south of Adelaide. A farm, actually.'

'Not more sheep?'

'No. No sheep, and apparently not much else either. Hurtle and family are moving to a place near there called Yankalilla, but he's had to take on a small farm as part of the package. There's nothing on it now except a small house, and we can have that until he gets himself sorted out there, or until we get a passage home. Whichever comes first...'

'A house?' I look round at the tiny room that has been our refuge for the last three months. 'A whole house?'

'Three bedrooms, I think! And a washhouse. There is one problem, though.'

I groan. 'I knew it! What's the catch?'

'Catch?' Eric frowns. 'What do you mean?'

'This is Hurtle we're talking about. I'm probably a bit more cynical than you, but I gather he likes to play his cards close to his chest.' Eric just blinks in acknowledgement. 'So, what's the problem?'

'There's no guarantee I'll get any work. Hurtle doesn't know anyone there, otherwise he would put in a good word for me. But apparently there are some other farms close by, and he reckons someone will take me on.'

'But not sheep farming.'

Eric grins. 'Not sheep farming! Right, we'd better start packing. We're moving on Saturday!'


*7th March 1950.*


*Dear Elsie and Alan,*

*Thanks Alan for your very welcome letter which arrived last Saturday.*

*Please go ahead with your plans regarding a house because we are not able to say anything definite yet. We would not like you to miss any chances on account of us, and as you say, if you do make a change, it would still be alright. Just one small room would do us. You should see our present bedroom, the hut. In any case, it would not be for long, we would try and get a house as soon as possible, though I know how very welcome you would make us. How are house prices at the present time? Perhaps you could give us some idea?*

*We are moving from here on Saturday, the business has been sold and somebody else is coming in on Monday.*

*We heard from the Immigration after almost 3 weeks, to say that we had mis-read their first letter, and if we wished to return we must pay our own passage, but we do not pay for the outward journey. We wrote again asking them to arrange a passage, but have not heard any more yet, that was a week ago.*

*Hurtle has bought a farm about 50 miles from Adelaide, nearer the coast. There is an old house on it which they will not be using and he proposes we go there for the time being. It is some miles out in the scrub, but I understand there is a bus into Adelaide once or twice a week. Goodness knows how we get our mail or groceries etc. I think there is a small place a few miles away, but we have no car or bicycle and Hurtle will not be on the farm for some time. I will be able to tell you more next time I write, if there is anywhere to post!*

*We have no wireless, and there won't be any daily paper, so this time we shall really know what it's like to be isolated, unless there is another farm nearby. I hope so or we shall have to live on dried milk unless Hurtle has some cows there. Please keep writing here until I can give you the new address.*

*Susan has gone to bed. I asked her if she had a message for you and she said* "Tell Auntie Elsie, has she got my bucket and spade?" *She sends her love and kisses to you both. I was listening to her and her latest boyfriend (3 years old) today – what a blood-thirsty conversation – going to chop each other's heads off. I think it's the butchery – Susan just loves watching them bring the meat in and chop it up.*

*We all went out to the pictures last Saturday, our first night out together since we came. Susan liked it but was very tired. The pictures don't start until 8pm and finish about 11 o'clock. She wouldn't go to sleep though. She made a few comments but nothing like as penetrating as Joan's! She has been once before in Adelaide and sat spellbound.*

*Do hope you will have luck in finding a nice house at reasonable cost. More chance than we have here anyway.*

*Much love to you both from*

*Mollie, Eric and Susan.*

# Part Three

## *Delamere*

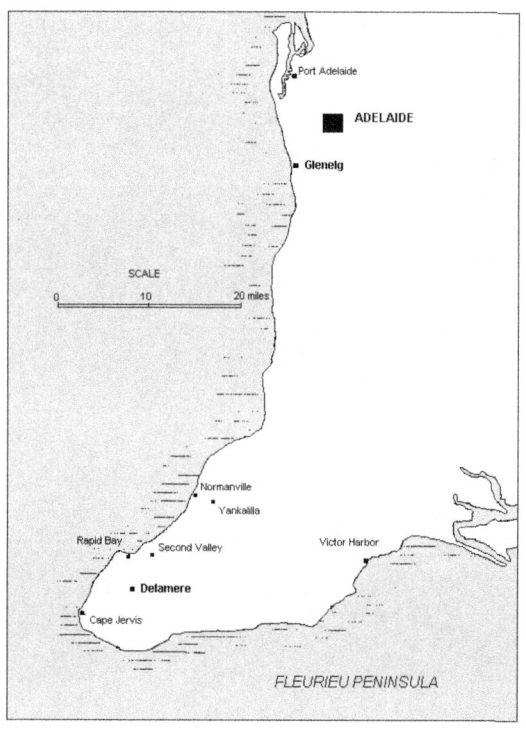

*11ᵗʰ March 1950 – Keith*

The sideboard is a heavy piece of furniture, and it is a struggle for the two men to lift it on to the back of the truck. I don't want to watch, partly out of concern that Eric might finally suffer an asthma attack. The other reason (which I keep to myself) is that I don't want to witness Mother's pride and joy tumble to the ground and end up as firewood. In the event, it is Hurtle who comes off worse.

'Give me a minute, will you mate?' He leans against the side of the vehicle, one hand clutching his chest.

'You okay?' says Eric.

Hurtle takes a couple of deep breaths before answering and then lets his arm drop. 'Never better. Least that's the worst lifted. Mollie, you did remember to empty it first, eh?'

Before I can answer, Eric hits back with some banter of his own. 'Empty it? I bet she's stuffed it full of rump steak and lamb chops.' He winks at me, then turns back to Hurtle. 'You ready to shift it into position now?'

I shake my head in amusement. I am glad to see my husband in good spirits and physical good health. He's been engaged in heavier manual labour over the last six months than he's been used to since demob, so it is obvious to me he is feeling fitter. But furniture shifting is a different demand to handling sheep carcasses. I remember how easily Hurtle lifted the trunk onto his shoulders on our arrival, and find myself doubting there will be a repeat performance today.

The two men climb on board the truck, and together they ease the sideboard up to rest flat against the back of the cab, leaving plenty of space behind for the rest of our family belongings. It is a warm Saturday evening in early autumn, and the plan is to load up the truck from the rooms behind the shop, and then stop one more night with Hurtle's sister Gladys before setting off at daybreak the next morning.

I've never really studied the truck before, having used it on just the one occasion last November. Remembering Hurtle has said another man will be coming with us on the journey, I feel I have to ask if he is sure we will all fit in?

'Course. Got to be done.' To Hurtle the logistics don't seem to be a problem. He throws one end of a rope over to Eric for him to tie the sideboard securely as he answers. 'Ken's riding shotgun for us on the way out in case we meet any abo's. Then we swap for the trip back.' He sees my expression and grins. 'Don't worry, girl. Abo's won't be any trouble, though we are going through their territory. More likely we'll pick a fight with a boomer. But I need Ken. Can't manage the drive both ways.'

I know that "abo's" means "aborigines" – Australia's indigenous black people, but I don't dare ask what Hurtle means by a "boomer". So as Eric appears content not to argue the point, I leave them to it and return to my own duties.

The next morning I am touched to see two friends we made at church, plus the minister and his wife, come to wave us off. It feels strange to be saying goodbye to someone once more, knowing it is unlikely we'll ever see them again. How curious it is that time and place have blurred my perception of life. I know we have only been living here a few short months, and yet it feels at least a year that we have spent in the company of these people with their smiles and their fellowship. The exchange of words is brief but warm, and I turn away quickly before the tears start to flow.

Eric helps me up into the cab next to Hurtle, clutching two gift-wrapped parcels as well as my raffia shopping basket. Next he swings Susan up so she can clamber over the seat, mildly protesting about having to sit on her mother's lap. Then it is Eric's turn, barely leaving a space a foot wide for the slimmer Ken to squeeze into. It is the passenger door that worries me. The elderly vehicle has suffered more than its fair share of "wear and tear" during Hurtle's ownership, and the door catch is not reliable. Eric has told me of two previous occasions when the door sprung open after the truck bounced over rough ground, and I don't envy Ken's current position. Hurtle also seems aware of it.

'Are we shut, Ken? Hooray – let's roll. Cosy in here, isn't it?'


Progress is slow. Hurtle's truck is laden with a mixed cargo: the sideboard, two mattresses, two plywood tea chests and any number of smaller boxes and packages (including Susan's toy pram) have all been covered in tarpaulin and firmly tied down with rope. Then there is the human content in the fragile cab. Also the road surface is not the best maintained – especially once we leave the main road towards Adelaide and start to head south and west for the coast. But first we have to skirt a huge expanse of lakes Hurtle tells us have been created from the Murray River. He seems happy to impress with his knowledge.

'This one here covers the best part of three hundred square miles, and the abo's used to think it had a monster swimming in it. One story says a white man was sailing on the lake when two great big hands came out of the water and grabbed the sides of the hull. The man fired his gun at the hands and they disappeared, but an abo sailing with him said he'd be made to suffer for that. Before he got ashore he was covered in blisters all over his body. Took him a long time to die...'

'Hurtle!' I can see Susan's brown eyes widen as she squirms round on my lap. 'Can we talk about something else? What's the lake called?'

'Sorry Moll. Biggest one is Lake Alexandrina. Go on – ask me who it's named after!'

'Well I suppose it's a woman called Alexandrina? So who was she?'

Hurtle slows the truck as he spots something moving off to his right. 'Wait a minute.'

Each of us turn our heads to watch the object approach. We have been travelling over an hour, and up to now the landscape either side of the road is still fairly flat, with the familiar mallee shrubs and scrubby trees sprinkled like green mould spores over a dusty brown blanket. As the truck settles into walking speed an oddly shaped animal comes bounding out of the undergrowth and onto the road directly in front of us. Larger than a sheep, it has long, powerful back legs that carry it swiftly across in two powerful springs before reaching the far side to our left. It has kept a perfectly straight course regardless of our approach. Then two more follow in its wake, slightly smaller, and a paler shade of brown than their leader. Hurtle battles with the gearbox and the truck picks up speed as the bounding figures are lost to view.

'Kangaroos!' I feel flushed with excitement. It is the first I have seen in the wild.

'Black bastards we call them. Sorry Moll. Just an expression. First one was a male. What we call a "boomer". Don't normally slow down but can't risk anything with all this on the truck today. Not your most popular animal to farmers like I used to be on account of them ruining our crops. What were you asking me?'

'Er – Alexandrina?'

'Oh yes. She was an English Princess. Then she became Queen and changed her name.' Hurtle turns his head to see if he has everyone's attention. Susan is still looking through the windscreen for kangaroos, but three faces are meekly awaiting his next pronouncement.

'To Victoria.' He grins at our obvious surprise. 'Yep. The Good Queen herself. That lake should have had its name changed a long time ago, but nobody got round to it yet.'

The long day continues in much the same vein, with Hurtle giving us the benefit of his Aussie upbringing – though I doubt many of his stories are anything more than fiction. There are several more incidents with kangaroos, and I spot some dark-faced men in small groups that Hurtle confirms are aborigines. There are also long silences (the slim Ken hardly speaks a word), and both Susan and I nod off on occasion, only to be rudely woken by the truck taking avoiding action from potholes, or from something on very powerful back legs.

The change in the countryside is quite marked as we reach the coast. We've grown accustomed to flat terrain and small scrubby undergrowth in the area south east of Adelaide, but now we are heading west, and the sea is closing in on both sides, although it is not always visible. As we leave the small town of Victor Harbor we find we have hills to cope with, and the old truck slows frequently as it struggles with the steeper slopes. There are dense trees all around us, and I find myself marvelling at what I would describe as forest, but in Australia is known as "bush". We are entering another world, but for some strange reason I can't yet appreciate, it feels like a good one.


We are standing on the veranda of our new home. A wooden structure clad in a form of galvanised iron sheeting, it was once a small farmhouse and served a basic need for at least a dozen Australian summers. Hurtle's plans for its future are still not clear, but his few comments about the buildings themselves have not been complimentary. Now, as he and Ken set off on their long journey back to Keith, the three of us are left alone to explore our new surroundings.

'Listen!' To me there is a welcome change in the stiff breeze.

Eric listens. Then he realises what my hearing has caught.

'Birdsong.'

'There! There's another. I can hear them but I can't see them.' I look up at trees that are over twice the height of any we have seen around the district of Keith. Branches awash with thick green leaves are waving their greetings in royal regard. Once I think I see a tiny splash of colour flitting among the shadows, and I point out the spot to Eric. He nods, but with a sleepy little girl in his arms he can do little more than smile.

The first task (on Hurtle's advice) is to scour the house for any signs of infestation. Nothing can be given anything like a permanent place until we have checked everywhere for animal, reptile or insect life where we don't want it. Eric says he found some "strange-looking beasties" in a sink in the kitchen, but he got rid of them before I saw any evidence.

Twelve months ago, if I had been looking for a house in Manchester and seen something like this, I would have refused to live in it. Mother would have thrown a fit. But after months living in that apology for a shed at the back of Hurtle's shop, this place feels so much more like a home. We have space, and while the floor and walls are bare of colour, I have a tingle of excitement thinking how I can run up some curtains and freshen it up to my liking. There is no electricity, of course, but we find a good supply of candles and several oil lamps that are still serviceable. All of which are put to good use fairly quickly as night follows soon after dusk, and it seems to me the house is so big that there are too many dark corners. Once we have set up Susan's bed and made it up, we get her settled easily and then tumble into our own, too tired even to think about food, although it has been several hours since we have eaten.

I cuddle my man in the gathering gloom of our new bedroom. 'Well darling, this is where it starts again. We have to make ourselves another home, even if it is only temporary. But I've got a feeling about this place. Maybe it's only the name, but there is something else... I think I'm going to like it here.'

*13ᵗʰ March 1950 – Delamere*

To my delight we wake to a proper dawn chorus. Our feathered neighbours are in full song at five o'clock, and the sense of freedom is overwhelming. I wipe away some tears as Eric puts his arms around me, reassuring me with his presence. For months he has left my side at first light most mornings, hurrying to his duties on Hurtle's farm. Now both of us are reluctant to move out from under the blanket.

In daylight it takes a while to come to terms with our new surroundings. What to do first? Hunger and thirst are the first demands to be attended to, so while Eric gets busy lighting the wood stove, I fill a couple of pans and a kettle with some brown tainted water from our outside tank, and set them ready to boil. We need clean water to drink and to cook with, then to wash in, and finally to help clean the whole interior. I am glad I have a good man about the house!

In fairness, our new home has been left in a reasonably good state, and the knowledge that it is totally ours to fix up how we want is a tremendous boost to our morale. For the first time since leaving Chorlton we finally have some independence. We know it might only be for a short time, and I know it sounds odd for me to say it now, but our house in Delamere gives me a sense of identity I have been missing. We are on our own, and we have some control over our immediate future. For once I can focus on the business of looking after my little family, and it doesn't seem to matter as much that we are so far away from the place I truly consider to be "home".

*Delamere, South Australia*
*16/3/50*

*Dear Elsie and Alan,*

*Thanks Elsie for your letter of the first. Well, as you see we have been busy removing. If you see a map of Australia, look for the long finger jutting out into the sea south of Adelaide, this place is almost at the tip.*

*We have a nice little house entirely surrounded by hills and bush country, but the village of Delamere (one shop and church) is 7 miles away, and that is the nearest point at which we can get a bus. The grocer etc comes from the village 2 or 3 times a week, but not to the house. We have to walk nearly a mile to a corner where each farm has a box, put our order in the box, and then go again to collect. The same with mail, so hope ours reaches you alright, we haven't had any yet since we left Keith last Sunday.*

*It is something like the Delamere we knew Alan, but not as nice. The trees are pretty thick but scraggy gums and awful looking things called yuccas, like stunted palms. The hills are very nice though and the sea is on 3 sides, we can see it in the distance, but cannot get to it as there are no roads and the bush is too thick. This is a sheep farm, the house in a little clearing and the bush right up to front and back doors. I find it rather eerie and the wind has been blowing hard and howling! There are two farms, both about half a mile away. Eric has been sawing wood at one this morning, and the people seem very nice. Hurtle's home will be at Yankalilla, about 19 miles away on another farm, but he is not there yet. I think he intends to do this one up and sell it again, as it is much too isolated for them to live here, but he had to take it from the fellow who bought the butchery, sort of part exchange. We hoped to visit Adelaide which is 52 miles off, but shall have to work out how to get to Delamere and also get back.*

*I have actually got a stove now, one in which we burn wood, and have been happy doing some baking and today roasted our first joint! Susan misses her little pals and has been busy colouring. Have just asked her if she has a message. The reply is still the same,* "Has Auntie Elsie got my bucket and spade?".

*We are quite enjoying this temporarily, but would not like it permanently. Still no word from the Immigration, but if we can get to Adelaide soon will go and see them. Just go ahead with your plans though.*

*Lots of love to you both.*

*Mollie & Eric & Susan*

The Farmhouse at Delamere

The house is my sanctuary. It *is* a bit of a wreck, I agree – but it is my palace, my refuge from a foreign world that will always be hostile. It is a fortress of relative safety where I can spend time with my daughter, and provide a home again for my hard-working husband. It is also the opportunity to do more of what I promised to do for Elsie: to write.

Without any duties to perform other than those relating to meals and laundry, I find it natural to put time aside each day and share the dining table with Susan on creative pursuits. While she sits at one end with a collection of paper and crayons, I sit at the other with my pen and my journal. I am determined to capture all I can about this most intrusive episode of our lives. I used to keep a diary as a girl, and once Susan is old enough I will encourage her to do the same, but the little leatherette bound volume Eric gave me at Christmas has not the capacity I need. This journal is therefore courtesy of George's vestry at Keith, and I simply pray there are enough pages inside for me to conclude our adventures here with a happy ending.

*18ᵗʰ March 1950 – Delamere*

It is much like any country lane I have ever experienced. In England I had a passion for the outdoors, and had been a keen walker despite my shortened leg. Younger brother Bert and I regularly went to the Lake District on church outings as teenagers, and there'd also been family trips for picnics to Cheshire, where Delamere Forest held great appeal. It is only natural for me to look for parallels with the English version, and as I explore the area nearest our new home with Susan, I find myself recalling a distant memory, taking my own mother's hand when we discovered a family of swans by the shore of Blakemere Lake. One of the birds seemed quite aggressive, and I've felt a little nervous around them ever since.

There are no swans in this part of the world, but there are some deep ruts in the lane, presumably caused by farm traffic. While the sun still retains a fair amount of heat, some clouds are gathering on the horizon to the north, and it is impossible for me to ignore the freshness of the air around me. Winter might be approaching, but to me it seems a great day to just enjoy being outdoors again.

Picking her way over the worst of the ruts in the lane, Susan begins to swing her arms vigorously and pretends to march like a soldier. Then she opens her mouth and bellows loudly.

'Who is the King of GLO-RY?'

I laugh, remembering the Harvest Festival we attended at the church in Keith just a short while ago. Susan watched while I practiced with the choir, and the little imp has since occasionally mimicked the choir mistress, waving her arms in dramatic fashion. Now something has inspired her to remember the key phrase from that one particular anthem – and to repeat it over and over again.

'Who is the King of GLO-RY?'

'Susan! You'll scare the birds out of the trees! What made you remember that, I wonder?'

She continues to swing her arms, but softens her voice almost to a whisper.

'Who is the King of Glo-ry?' Then she stops as something catches her attention. 'Look at the flowers, Mummy!'

I look. There is a field full of a large leafy crop to our right. Dotted among them are occasional splashes of white where the crop has flowered, and at first I think it is these that have caught Susan's eye. But at the edge nearest them the land has been left to nature, and standing taller than the scrubby thick grass are several groups of flowers with a yellow centre circled by large white petals tinged with pink.

'Oh! Michaelmas daisies!' Again I find myself reminded

of the English countryside so far away. 'How lovely to see them here.'

We go closer to the floral display, marvelling at the clean vivid colours. A strong breeze has developed during our walk, and the sturdy wild flowers appear to dance and bow before us like excited Lilliputians, basking in the attention of the sun as it peers past scudding clouds.

Then a faint male voice is carried over the wind. I look up, alarmed to see a man I take to be a farmer waving his arm as he approaches from a distance across that same field.

'Come along, Susan! I think we may be trespassing.'

I grasp Susan's hand just in time to prevent her trying to pull one of the flowers out of the ground, but then the farmer calls again. This time he is close enough for me to make out what he says.

'Wait! Let me help.'

We stand in the lane, watching as the man draws closer. Of average height and build, and with untidy blonde hair, he is dressed in the same kind of worn and frayed work clothes that all the Australian men I've met seem to favour: short-sleeved shirt and baggy cotton pants with heavy work boots. The deep tan on his face and forearms is testimony to a life spent outdoors, and while his facial expression is impassive, the spoken word implies friendship. 'You must be careful. Beauty and danger are often the good companions.'

The accent is *not* Australian, and while I try to place it the man stops at the edge of the field, standing in the same spot where Susan had been just moments earlier. Then he stamps the earth several times and stoops towards the flowers, clapping his hands loudly. Seemingly satisfied, he straightens up and turns to us. 'My apologies. I am not wishing to alarm you, but sometimes there are snakes, you know?'

I feel myself blush. 'Thank you. Yes, of course. I'm

sorry. I should have thought. It was the flowers. They look so lovely, and they remind me of home.'

'The *tusensköna*? You are from England? Yes? That is good. I and my wife, we come from Sweden. We are each strangers in a foreign country! Here – you must have a gift.'

The man produces a sharp penknife from his pocket, and bends down to cut the stems of several of the colourful daisies close to the ground, before handing some to us both. He enquires how far we are intending to walk, and I explain we have recently moved in to an old farmhouse. The Swedish farmer nods enthusiastically, seeming ever more pleased he has a new neighbour.

'I think he said his name was Jacobson. There's just him and his wife, so I told him you were looking to do casual labour on the farms, and he said he could probably use your help as his potatoes are nearly ready for harvesting'

Eric nods. 'He was right to warn you about the snakes. It's the vibrations they can sense rather than noise, so heavy work boots are a better line of defence than what you had on your feet!'

His own pair are sitting outside on the veranda, doused liberally with fine dust from a day's wood-cutting. We are sitting at our table, and I watch as he finishes off his dinner of minced lamb and carrots. A glass jar takes pride of place in the centre, where a colourful floral bouquet adds a welcome splash of colour to our Spartan surroundings.

'So what's Susan doing? I can hear her talking to someone.'

'She's found a cat. Didn't you see him when you came in? Or perhaps I should say he found her! He came out of nowhere as we returned from our walk. Just gave a loud "miaow" and rubbed himself up against her like they do. Took no notice of me at all. Would you like some more?'

I pick up his empty plate as Eric changes the subject.

'I've been thinking – about this problem with the immigration people. We're still assuming we'll have to make our own arrangements unless they tell us any different. I'm not waiting for a reply any longer, and it is possible something got lost in the post with us moving here. The only way to find out properly where we stand is to go and see them in person, in Adelaide. We'll have to go there to book our passage anyway. There's a daily bus service in the mornings from the village, and Joe says he can run us down there. Coming back might be more of a problem, but he did say the grocer might be able to bring us with him when he does his round in the afternoon.'

'That's all very well,' I say, returning from the kitchen with a full plate. 'But we can't get everything done in a day. We're going to need to stay somewhere and make the most of a day
or more. Hotels cost money, Eric – and if we end up having to pay for our passage to England, we're going to have to save every penny we can.'

Eric nods, pausing to digest another mouthful. 'That's where George comes in.'

'George?'

'Alcock. Before we left Keith he gave me some information about the Returned Soldiers League.'

'What's that? He never mentioned anything to me.'

'Charitable institution for ex-servicemen, like me. George reckons I'd qualify for some assistance, even if it's just a few days bed and board. I'm going to use the phone at Joe Guy's tomorrow, as long as you're okay with the idea?'

I take a breath and give the suggestion some thought. 'Okay love. So long as we're not having to all sleep in a hammock, let's do it. We need all the help we can get.' I look out of the window at the dancing trees. 'I'm going to have to get Susan to put that cat outside and get her off to bed. The wind seems to be getting worse – and I'm sure it's going to rain.'

Susan with Dandy

*23ʳᵈ March 1950 – Delamere*

Looking back at those early months of 1949 before we left Manchester, I realise how ignorant I was of what the weather could be like in Australia. Then I thought it was a place of constant sunshine, where everyone walked around in short sleeves and cotton dresses. I had no idea that the seasons existed in much the same way as England, but were reversed and more extreme. I also learned there could be wide variations of weather patterns across South Australia, even within the relatively small area south and east of Adelaide that we came to know.

After the flat, sparse land around Keith we had seen during the Aussie summer, we were now living in a more lush area close to the sea. The peninsula that includes our farm is subject to coastal breezes and a fresher atmosphere than we have been used to. There are hills and valleys, and vast acres filled with trees that I soon learn are commonly known as "Stringybark", with some looking very much like our English oak. Eric often works at a small saw mill not far from our house for a chap named Joe Hooper. There is never any shortage of work or raw materials as there is a constant demand for timber in Australia's construction industry. It is while Eric is working for Joe in these early days that I learn how different things can be in our new homeland, as the autumn months bring a change in the weather.

'Dandy's found something, mummy.'

'What, dear?' I am standing on a chair at one of the windows, trying to use my tape measure to check the width of the frame.

'It's very small, but it moves very fast.'

I stop what I am doing, my mind switching from thoughts of curtain material to thoughts of vermin. Susan's new cat has probably found a field mouse, but is it inside the house?

'All right, darling.' I step carefully off the chair and cross over to the table to write down the width measurement. 'Whereabouts is Dandy now?'

'In there.' Susan points at the doorway that leads to our washhouse.

'Right then, let's have a look at what he's found.'

It isn't a mouse. I expect to see Dandy chasing a furry

grey thing on four legs round and round the floor. Instead he is sat on the shelf next to the large trough we have yet to use for washing our clothes. His ginger tail is twitching with excitement while his body remains still, large eyes focussed on a tiny brown creature squatting at the far end.

'Oh, my goodness! It's a frog. How on earth did that get there?'

I soon find out. I quickly drag the trough out of the back door and tip it up to encourage the frog to escape. Dandy happily joins us and chases the little thing out of its hiding place and into the long grass. Thinking it best to swill out the trough before use I drag it back inside under the tap and turn the lever. The water that spurts out brings two more frogs with it! I scream, and Susan follows my example at an even higher pitch.

The creatures are probably as shocked as I am, having endured a dramatic journey from our outside water tank through the connecting pipe to our washhouse. I'm not happy to play host to a family of frogs, and after recovering from my surprise at their appearance, make another trip outside to encourage them back to their natural environment. But moments later we have another (more welcome) interruption.

Our next visitor is announced in the normal way by a knock at our front door. Even at Grace's house there was never an occasion when someone called without notice. This isn't like our home back in Manchester where we could expect delivery of a parcel or telegraph, or where a neighbour might drop round to share some gossip. As far as I am aware, we are at least a mile away from anyone else, and I am certainly not expecting Hurtle to pop back for a chat.

So I am especially surprised when I open the door to find a woman standing there, carrying a basket covered with a teacloth. She is possibly twenty years older than me, with long blonde hair swept up in an untidy bun, and dressed in what looks like a man's shirt and working trousers. A hesitant smile appears on thin lips. For a moment I think she might be a gypsy trying to sell me a bundle of heather.

'Good day to you,' says the stranger.

'Er... Good day?'

'We are neighbours. You and I are very close. Welcome to Delamere!'

'Oh, my goodness!' I say for the second time that day. 'You must be Mrs Jacobson!'

'*Ja*,' says my visitor with a broad smile. 'I think you may like *fika*. May I..?'

And so my first human visitor steps over the threshold. This is indeed the wife of the farmer I met only a day or so ago. Her husband has obviously told her of our meeting, so she made it her business to introduce herself, and to bring gifts too. Spotting Susan by the table she drops onto one knee to greet her properly, which impresses me. Susan produces a shy smile for our guest, who has her face at the same level. The two shake hands in solemn fashion.

'So today we are all good friends, *ja*?' says Mrs Jacobson, now standing to shake my own hand.

It feels so formal, meeting a neighbour like this, and I'm not sure what kind of hospitality I should offer. Is it the right thing to do to offer a cup of tea? (More to the point, is there enough water in my kettle not to risk another intrusion of frogs?) But Mrs Jacobson is already in charge: she places her basket on our table and removes the cloth with a flourish. Inside are a gaudily coloured biscuit tin and a glass jar containing a brown powdery substance.

'These are for you,' she announces with pride. 'A little something we do in my own country. You drink coffee?'

'Oh! Well, no – not very often. That is, I usually drink tea.' I feel my cheeks redden to sound so rude and so English. I haven't tried coffee for at least a year, and don't like the bitter taste. But this gracious Swedish lady does not appear to take offence.

'Today you will like it. We call it *fika*, but it is not good unless with a pastry.' She puts the jar down by the basket and pulls out the biscuit tin. 'These are *semla* buns. They taste better with coffee. In Sweden we have *fikarast* – what you would call a coffee break, yes?'

It is the beginning of a very special friendship. That afternoon passes too quickly as I find myself enjoying the company of another female. I am playing hostess in my own house, and yet this neighbour is also hosting me. She shows me how to make her special kind of coffee with the addition of an egg, a combination I would never have imagined before. To my surprise it is a taste I find fairly pleasant, and is not as bitter as I expect. And the dough buns that she brings are eaten while they sit in warm milk – a tradition connected with the religious festival of Lent. My sweet tooth is instantly appeased, and Susan asks for more – just like Oliver.

Mrs Jacobson laughs when I tell her about the frogs, and she promises to get her husband to call round and put something in our water tank to get rid of them. She tells me they bought their farm a little over ten years ago, having first migrated from Sweden in 1926. They have a grown up daughter living in Adelaide, but sadly she lost another child to polio many years ago, not long after arriving in Australia. Would they consider going back to Sweden? Mrs Jacobson pulls a face before replying.

'No. It is not the same. The politics there, as they are in Europe, are not for us. You are English so you would not understand. In Sweden we were good workers. We were farming and the Party, it was supposedly helping the workers. You know Lenin?'

I nod, suddenly nervous of our topic of conversation.

'Communism is very strong in Sweden. Very strong. But it is not accepted by everyone as you will know. Look what happened in Europe... Ugh! We will not go there, will we? I must go now before the rain comes.'

And so as abruptly as she arrived, Mrs Jacobson makes her exit. She warns me the rain will be heavy when it comes, but will soon pass. Then she hurries away up the lane to her farm, and I eye the black clouds building above us with suspicion as the trees moan in the gathering wind.

Our washhouse at the rear

Back home in Manchester I cannot recall taking notice of the times of sunrise or sunset. I remember on summer nights we would often marvel at how light it still seemed at ten o'clock. But back then I lived in a city lit with street lamps, and on winter evenings I was accustomed to seeing cars and lorries light up the roads as those who had been on the day shift made their journey home. It was routine; an accepted fact that as the working day drew to a close we would flick a switch and illuminate our world. But the changing seasons in Australia paint a very different picture.

With so many men working outdoors it is necessary to

adjust their hours according to the amount of daylight available. March in Delamere sees the sun setting earlier each night as summer gives way to autumn, and so I know Eric will have to finish work around six o'clock, with the sun slipping below the horizon shortly after. But on the day Mrs Jacobson pays her first visit the darkness begins so much earlier. I feel a momentary panic that I will be late preparing a meal for Eric. Then I look at my watch and am amazed to see it is only a little after three. The threatening cloud cover makes it seem a lot later. While I have to forego my plans to measure up for curtain material, I still feel confident time is on my side in the kitchen department – even if it has to be done with the assistance of a kerosene lamp.

The thought does cross my mind that Joe Hooper might send Eric home early on account of the fading light. But unlike our little farmhouse the saw mill has a battery electricity supply, so I guess there is little chance of that happening if it is just a matter of switching on a few lights to continue working a bit longer.

I am nervously filling a pan of water when the rain arrives, and all thought of frogs goes out of my head. It is as if the Almighty has opened a vastly bigger tap immediately over our roof, and the roar of that first deluge shocks me so much that I drop the pan and scream for the second time that day. Susan comes running into the washhouse and flings her little arms around the top of my legs. I clutch her shoulders for support and crane my neck to look at our roof. It seems to be still intact, and we are not in any immediate danger. But the corrugated sheets above me are trembling against the beams with the force of the raindrops and the noise is horrendous. I can hear the faint voice of a child crying from a distance. Then I realise she is scrabbling at my waist, desperate for her mother's attention.

After another glance at the roof and walls of the

washhouse for any sign of collapse, I grab Susan's hand and pull her with me into the main part of the house in the hope of a better refuge. We find the relative safety of my bed and tumble into it, clinging to each other for mutual support. I cannot believe the speed at which the weather has changed, despite the warning from my Swedish neighbour. Here inside our bedroom the noise seems slightly less – or it may be the rain has subsided a little, or perhaps my ears have merely adjusted themselves to the volume. Susan buries her head in my breast while my thoughts turn to Eric. Will he have been caught in the rain outside? Could there be floods? Might he have got lost in the bush? Then I find my daughter's priorities have taken an altogether different direction.

'Mummy? What about Dandy?'

'What, darling?'

'Where's Dandy? He's not here.'

She sniffles silently and glares at me with accusing damp eyes. I sit up and stare back at her in the lamp-lit gloom.

'Susan, he's a big cat. He'll be absolutely fine. He's probably been through lots of nights like this. Here, dry your eyes.'

I still have to raise my voice against the din coming from above, which feels all wrong when trying to soothe a child's fears. But Susan is having none of it. She ignores my proffered handkerchief and flings herself off the bed in search of her precious animal friend.

'Dandy! Dandy!'

Right now trying to stop my daughter from worrying about her cat is about as much use as wishing for world peace. With some reluctance I follow her into each of our four rooms and check every corner for a sign of the missing animal. The first tour of the house does not yield a result. I have to physically prevent Susan from going out into the rain to check the outhouses. Thankfully a more thorough search finds him hiding behind a box of toys underneath her bed. While he shows no interest in leaving his refuge for the moment, I leave Susan there in a slightly better mood and return to the washhouse to retrieve my large saucepan.

One benefit of looking for Susan's cat is that I also have the opportunity to check for leaks. It is a relief to find no sign of anything serious – just three spots where water is dripping with any frequency. I am pleased Mother's sideboard has been spared, and I only have to move our table aside and place a bucket on the floor to contain the worst of it. Sensing the noise level is receding a little, I check that both child and cat are reunited and then resume work in the kitchen.

Our meal is prepared and I am just feeding Susan when I hear what sounds like a muffled explosion over the incessant roaring of raindrops. I haven't the slightest doubt this long drawn-out rumble is something more familiar. Susan's eyebrows shoot up as she looks at me in alarm.

'Not to worry, darling,' I say. 'God's only moving his furniture round.'

Susan chews at her dinner and considers this suggestion.

'Why is he doing it now?'

'Because it's easier to do it when the rain is so noisy.'

She seems satisfied with this explanation and returns her attention to spooning up mashed potato. Before the food reaches her mouth the whole room is flooded in the brightest light imaginable, blazing through our windows in a momentary assault. Every detail of the floor, walls and roof are thrown into stark definition as shadows flee in retreat. A flash of ginger fur close to the ground catches the corner of my eye as Dandy hurries back to his under-bed sanctuary. Susan's interest in her mashed potato takes a temporary diversion, but thankfully not because of the cat.

'Oh, what's God up to NOW?' she says crossly.

As thunderstorms go it is the worst (and longest) I ever

experienced. Hours pass and the deafening noise fills our ears well into the evening as it becomes clear Eric will not be home while the weather is so severe. I alternate my time in a constant round of cuddling up to my daughter, emptying buckets and staring out of the window. I am in awe of the power of nature as dozens of lightning flashes lay siege to the army of trees not twenty feet away, their thrashing branches seemingly ablaze in a white fire that makes me think we are at the very edge of Hell. At any moment I expect to see a huge demonic figure burst through the maelstrom and hurl a thunderbolt at our puny little shelter.

Strangely, Susan ignores the frequent flashes but seems happy enough to try and sleep in my bed. At least, until the lightning passes she remains with her head under the covers and her eyes tight shut. I keep two lights burning, one in the main room on the off-chance Eric might welcome it should he attempt to get back home. The other is on the upturned tea chest next to our bed, and while I lie there listening to the storm fading into the distance, I watch the shadows flickering in the lamplight around me.

The rain remains constant, a never-ending presence battering the thin roof and walls around us. I think back to previous nights when I was unable to sleep for any reason. I remember that first night aboard ship, separated from Eric and wondering about our future. There was a weakly lit bulb in the bulkhead above our bunks, presumably there for safety reasons in the event of an incident at sea. It occurred to me then how primeval our situation was: keeping a light burning at times of danger. I thought of sailors at sea, looking for guidance to keep them from being dashed onto rocks. I thought of cavemen lighting fires to keep predators at bay. My husband is a religious man and often talks of Jesus Christ lighting our path. Is he safe enough out there somewhere? Is he sheltering from the rain and thinking about his wife and child? Where on earth is he?

As the night grows older the rain slows and then stops altogether. But not before one bucket has overflowed in the living room. In our kitchen a mess of potatoes and cold soup sits unloved and forgotten under a teacloth. Sleep somehow comes to me as the wind that battled the neighbouring trees gives up its fight and looks for conquests elsewhere. Our un-curtained windows are aglow with sparkling daylight when I wake to a kiss from my beaming errant husband.

I smile as my world returns to normal. 'Eric, darling – I have got such a lot to tell you!'


*29ᵗʰ March 1950, at the Returned Soldiers League – Adelaide*

'Where are we going to live now, Mummy?'

'We're going to the Big City, Susan! But only for a little while. Don't worry.'

Eric puts in his own two penn'orth: 'Hey Suey! Think of it as an adventure. You'll have so much to tell that cat of yours when you get back!'

We are on a bus, Susan and I together with Eric in sole occupation of the seat in front, and our suitcases on the rack above our heads. There are only two other people aboard, probably both farmers, plus the driver. The three buildings that make up the "township" of Delamere are slowly receding behind us and now the Veale family are on the road again. This time our destination will be reached inside three hours instead of six weeks, and on this occasion we are not going to be looking around us with rose-coloured spectacles.

Since "the night of the storm" we have done a lot of talking. Without the daily pressures of Eric working on Hurtle's farm we find it much easier to share our thoughts and opinions. Paid work is frequently available on a casual basis, and between jobs he has even found time to put up a simple swing for Susan to play on – when she isn't occupied with crayons or with Dandy. But it feels so comfortable to be a family again. The three of us walked up the lane to get to know our Swedish neighbours better. We learned more about their personal history, and about the neighbourhood. They in turn have their views on the difficulties faced by new settlers in Australia. Mr Jacobson was already a farmer before he reached these shores, and his own experiences were completely different from Eric's. But he understands our dilemma. Yes, there are plenty of jobs if you know where to look, and for a single man with no responsibility the possibilities are endless. For a young family needing permanent housing and access to a school it is a different matter. We have spent a long time discussing every option we think might be open to us if we stay in Australia. We have looked at our savings and reckoned up what it might cost if we have to pay for a passage home ourselves. Finally we are taking ourselves off to the Big City to try and settle things once and for all.

'You'll like this, Mollie.'

I tear my eyes away from the turquoise blue sea to our left, and see that Eric's attention has been caught by something in the newspaper he picked up at the store before our departure.

'What?'

Eric winks at me and then quotes from his paper. 'The headline reads *Australians too fond of luxuries*.'

I stifle a laugh and glance across at the backs of our fellow passengers, wondering if they might have taken offence. Neither turns round, and with the noise of the engine being louder for them than for us at the back of the bus, I feel some relief.

Eric continues to quote from the paper unabashed. '*Mr Ramsay, who is president of the SA branch of International Affairs, said the daring rate of migration Australia was attempting had never been surpassed by any nation. "With this population increase, which is very necessary for Australia, we need a big capital development program,"* said Mr Ramsay. *"But we can have this only if we are willing to forgo some of our luxuries."*'

We look at each other in bemusement. Luxuries have been almost totally absent from our lives for the last five months. To us it is a treat simply to sit on a rickety old bus with the knowledge that we can look forward to a few days together as a family. But we also know to what the newspaper refers. In those same pages there are any number of advertisements for costly electrical goods like radiograms and refrigerators – anything around a hundred pounds each – as well as other furniture at prices well out of our budget.

'Any non-luxury property for sale in the real estate section?' I ask, already knowing the answer.

'If you have to ask the price, you can't afford it,' is Eric's initial response. 'Or there's this one in some place called Gawler: *Five rooms and kitchen, sunroom and sleepout. All electric, stone and brick, garden laid out, fruit trees etc, and in good position. Suit retired butcher. Vacant possession. £2,250.*'

'Really? Suit retired butcher?'

'Sorry Mollie,' he grins. 'I made that bit up!'

'Fair enough, wise guy. Come on, hand it over. I want to see if John Martin's has any offers on.'

I have two reasons to visit the big store on Rundle Street. Firstly I am sure their drapery section will help solve my quest to put up curtains in our new home. The second is that Mrs Jacobson has told me her daughter Kitty works in the grocery department, and I have been given charge of a personal letter to deliver there. When it comes to it I fail on both counts: the material is just too expensive, and Kitty is off ill with a severe toothache, so I leave the letter with her manager.

Adelaide arrives in an explosion of the senses: after many months in sleepy countryside areas I am hardly prepared for the noise and pace of city life. I keep a tight hold of Susan as we get off the bus at Victoria Square and head for our accommodation less than a quarter of a mile away in Angas Street. Like Manchester there are trams and buses besides commercial vans and a good many private cars, but the streets are so much broader. I try to concentrate on Eric striding purposefully in front with the suitcases, but it is difficult not to be distracted. We are all buttoned up against a cold wind, and yet the temperature is in the mid sixties. I see some people getting off a tram wearing cotton dresses and thin jackets, and then realise we must have finally "acclimatised" to the Aussie weather!

Once settled in our room at the veterans' hostel we are determined to get straight on with our quest. So it is back to the Square for a short tram ride up King William Street to North Terrace and the area we first explored back in November. The Immigration Department is like many other public buildings I have experienced, and the result is depressingly familiar. After finding the right office on the fourth floor, Eric asks to speak to Mr Shiner, the man who signed each of the letters we have received to date. But we are out of luck (as usual). Mr Shiner is in a meeting and cannot take any appointments until the following day. So Eric books himself in for a morning slot and we leave the building determined to do something to cheer ourselves up. We find what we need at the Mayfair with Bing Crosby in *A Connecticut Yankee in King Arthur's Court* – just the ticket!


'I could have told you all this in a phone call, mate.'

'Not so easy where we are. I wanted to avoid any confusion.'

'No confusion on my part, Mr Veale. You're all entitled

to stay, and Lord knows there's plenty of opportunities for you out here. But if you're not suited, then you're free to go. But you do it under your own steam, if you get me? In other words, you book your own passage home. Not up to us.'

Mr Shiner has receding hair and a red face, as Susan has already pointed out in a voice loud enough for him to hear. I can't see Eric's, but the back of his ears do look a little pink from where I am sitting. The two men are clearly frustrated with each other, and as the Aussie official once again reminds Eric of the option of applying through the Housing Trust, I can sense it is time to go.

'Yes, yes I know! Anything up to two years wait – I've already looked at that.'

'That's for rental. They're only about eighteen hundred to buy and all you need is a twenty per cent deposit. Then the payments are very affordable – if you have a job...'

'All right Mr Shiner.' Eric turns round and heads straight for the door. 'Thanks for your time. Come on, Mollie. We're wasting our own time here.'

We retreat to the one part of Adelaide where we feel relatively at home – Elder Park. It hasn't changed – just a few more leaves on the ground. The last time we were there those same leaves were young and newly formed. Seeing so many of them drifting over the grass seems appropriate somehow. Like them we arrived in the spring, confident of good times ahead. Like them we now feel used up and cast aside, ready to drift in the wind with no idea where we might end up. Susan senses the sombre mood and remains quiet for a moment while Eric and I face up to our situation.

'You could do all right on your own,' I suggest.

'Don't be silly. I'm not on my own.'

'I just meant– '

'I know what you meant, but it doesn't count for anything now. I know you don't think much of Australia, I understand that completely and I'm inclined to agree with you. I can't have you and Susan roughing it any more. This isn't what either of us signed up for when we got married.'

We walk on in silence for a moment, watching the swans on the lake without really seeing them. Then Susan has a suggestion.

'Can we go to the zoo?'

Eric and I look at her, then at each other. As usual, our daughter has a way of breaking the tension and bringing a smile to our lips.

'Susan, that is a very good idea,' I say. 'You remembered us talking about it on the bus, didn't you? But I don't think we can manage that today, darling. Mummy and Daddy still have some things to do this afternoon, but I promise you we WILL go to the zoo tomorrow, if you can be a very good girl a little while longer today.'

How easy it is to reassure our daughter. I so wish I could swap places with her right now. There she is, content to walk in the park with her parents knowing we will provide all that she needs, no matter what. But one of those parents is me, and I feel so nervous about what might happen next. If ever I need my own mother's advice it is right now. As we walk on in silence that day, with a scattering of leaves across our path, I feel myself transported to Southern

Cemetery again. To the graveside with Joan and Dr Faustus. *What will be, shall be.*

But this time it isn't possible to leave things to fate. A decision has to be made. Eric and I already knew what the Immigration officer would say before we got there. We just needed to hear it face to face. And I knew my husband held out just the slimmest of hopes that speaking to someone might lead to an alternative solution. Could there *still* be a way of pursuing his dream?

Eric leads us all the way up to the bandstand that the locals call the rotunda, and we turn to look back at the view down to the lake before he speaks again. 'So what do we do now, Mollie? Do we try something else? Or do we go back?'

There it is – the question I have been dreading. Somehow I know Eric will want it to be *my* decision. His own plans have come to nought. Now it is up to me to fix them.

But somewhere across the ether there are other forces at work. Perhaps my prayers really do achieve divine intervention as I hear another voice pipe up at my side.

'I want to go home!'

Hearing Susan's plaintive little protest at that moment will stay with me forever. She is voicing what is in her own heart, and yet in truth it is also something shared by all three. My eyes meet Eric's and I can see he understands. He bends down and bundles his daughter up onto his hip.

'And so we shall, Susan. So we shall.'


*Adelaide 30/3/50*


*Dear Elsie and Alan,*


*Here we are in the Big City after what seems like a year instead of 5 months. It is lovely to be amongst* the bustle, see the trams and laid out gardens, and of course the shops!

The first news is that we have booked our passage to return home, but this will not be until August 24th, every ship on all lines is booked up. We went to the Immigration Dept yesterday. They do not fix your passage home, nor can they do anything for you when you are nominated. After you arrive here they have finished.

We shall not get our mail until next Monday. We came here Tuesday morning, left home 6.20am in a truck to go 7 miles to Delamere, got the bus at 7.15 and got here at 10.30am. We are staying at the R.S.L. Club (Returned Soldiers League). It is a lovely place, but shall have to move out tomorrow to a private house for the next 3 nights.

Poor little Susan is bewildered with all our changes, and we have to keep reassuring her we are going back to her toys at Delamere. We took her to the Zoo this afternoon, she loved it and wanted to bring one of the penguins back with her. The shops are full of beautiful Easter Eggs, so Susan will be able to have a nice one this year.

If we sail on August 24th, it will be in the Orcades, a new ship which we are told is really beautiful. It is due in London on Sept 18th, so it is much quicker than the Esperance, but we shall have to go to Melbourne to get on it as it does not call here. As far as I know we shall remain at Delamere in the meantime, though of course you never know what may happen. Four and a half months is a long time and something else may turn up and we may stop in Australia after all so go ahead with any plans you may have. Whatever happens my heart will always be in England, but I must pray for what will be best for all of us.

*How I will be thinking of you at Easter. Will Joan be home? It seems all wrong here with the leaves falling and autumn in the air. It has been just nice today – about 70 degrees and a cool wind.*
*God bless you both always. Much love from*

*Mollie, Eric and Susan*

*10ᵗʰ April 1950 – Delamere*

It is as if a milestone has passed. Barely a month after leaving Keith and I find life has altered so much. Our passage home is now booked, and I should be feeling elated that we can start to plan our return to family and some sort of normality. The old Mollie would be dancing with excitement, but this new girl who has taken me over has taught me to be more cautious. Things could change yet.

And then, I've recognised something in me that was never there before: I'm starting to like it here. It is Mrs Jacobson who has made me realise.

'The grapefruit are all harvested now, of course. It was a good year for them. You should have seen the blossom in September last. That is usually a good sign for the crop.'

'I've never seen a grapefruit tree. What colour is the blossom?

'White. The leaves are dark green. Look – those are our trees there.'

We are sheltering behind the farmhouse as the weather has turned very damp and showery. I have been admiring a well-established hydrangea bush outside her washhouse door and a lilac tree that has not yet flowered. Eric is helping Mr Jacobson dig some potatoes and Susan is somewhere playing with Dandy and his less adventurous half-brother Sandy. We discovered both cats belonged to the Swedish farmers. Even before we arrived that morning a little crate has been set aside for us, full of tomatoes, grapefruit, mushrooms and (of course) potatoes. What a charitable couple we have for neighbours! I am in a very contented mood as Mrs Jacobson and I peer through the drizzle at the pair of mature fruit trees nestling behind a small barn.

'Heavens, they do look healthy. I can't wait to see them flower this year!'

'Yes, it is a good display. But I think you will miss it, too, Mrs Veale?'

I look at my neighbour and see her quizzical expression. Then I realise what she means.

'Of course! September – we'll be on the way to England...' I remember the voyage on *Esperance Bay*, and the weeks we spent in that artificial world long ago. 'I'm so sorry. I forgot.'

'No apology please. But a shame we have so little time as neighbours.'

She goes looking for a petrol iron that is no longer needed. I feel deeply touched by Mrs Jacobson's generosity, trying to help us make our present home more comfortable. Her own house has electricity produced by a wind-powered battery. She even has a wireless, which makes me jealous, picturing the two of them sat next to their log fire listening to *The Man in Black* – a drama series from the BBC they both like. We find ourselves discussing actors we fancy, and I tell her of my obsession with Robert Donat.

'It's all in the voice,' I say. 'He suffers from asthma, like Eric, and there's something about his tone...' I find myself blushing, and she laughs.

'I know! I know. I do remember him in *The Thirty Nine Steps*? Such a charmer! And not bad-looking – for an English man!'

With the Jacobson's

We stand there in her kitchen, giggling like schoolgirls, and it feels so natural. I am relaxed in her company, which is curious because she is that much older than me, foreign and also an atheist. We have so little in common in our lives and yet a bond has started to show.

Another subject that has altered my view of life after our visit to Adelaide is the urgent need to save money. We have been putting some away already and have paid a deposit for our fare home of forty five pounds. Eric tells me that would be about thirty six pounds in English money. The balance of around one hundred and fifty in Australian currency will have to be paid in four months, and that does *not* include the cost of shipping the sideboard back – so we have a lot on our plate. Hurtle still owes us a fair bit from all the long hours Eric put in at the farm, and so far he has been busy with removing and getting set up in Yankalilla. He has promised Eric he 'will see him right' once that is over and done with, so I'm hoping it will improve our bank balance soon.

Without the help of our new friends we would struggle. Eric does get regular work at the sawmill with the Hooper's. They are a nice family; Joe's son Kevin is newly married and also works at the mill. He looks after the transport and has been wonderful offering lifts to the store at Delamere. I just wish they had been able to help at Easter, as I should have loved to attend the service at the little church there. Alas – another atheist family! I'm not complaining though. The people here all seem quite cheerful. Everyone appears to look out for their neighbours, and all seem to get on. But Eric did come back from the mill one day with a story I found hard to swallow.

'Did you know Jacobson might have a drink problem?'

'No! Really? Why do you say that?'

Eric sat down at the table, a big smile on his face. 'Kevin says he did an odd thing at the weekend. You know the Jacobson's have a car?'

I nodded. They keep it in a shed and rarely seem to use it. Petrol has only just stopped being rationed, and I assume they are just being careful. They have been very kind supplying a small can with the iron for me to use.

'Well, Jacobson went to Normanville on Saturday, I think. Not sure why. Got friends there, probably. Anyway Sunday morning Kevin was up at the store and was passing that big dairy farm when he spotted the car at the side of the road.' Eric paused as I put his dinner in front of him and then sat down with my own. 'It was perched on top of the milk stand, three feet off the ground! Lord knows how he managed to get it up there!'

I knew what Eric was describing. The farm is off the road leading to Delamere, much bigger than Jacobson's. Milk churns would normally be placed on a wooden stand at the side of the road, which is at a height where they can be transferred easily onto the back of the milk wagon – so it is clearly not a likely spot for a car to be found.

'How did he do it?' said Eric. 'Kevin and Joe reckon he must have taken a shortcut off the Main Road, but that's not something you'd do if you were sober. So – they reckon Jacobson had a skinful in town Saturday night and ended up going a bit astray on his way home!'

Swedish, communist, atheist and a possible drink problem – what strange neighbours we have made friends with. But they are our closest friends, and life could be so much more difficult without them. We have never asked them about the car, so it will just have to remain a mystery.

*Delamere, S.A.*
*11/4/50*

*Dear Elsie and Alan,*

*Thank you both for your letters. We received the one from Elsie just after we returned from Adelaide last week and Alan's yesterday. Susan has informed me that she wants to be called Beverley. I couldn't think why until I remembered reading aloud Auntie Elsie's letter referring to 'Beverley growing into a nice girl'. Susan desperately wants to be good but often falls down! She looked very grown up today ironing her socks and hair ribbons with a real iron (Petrol type).*

*I'm so glad you had a nice week with your German friends, it would be interesting to talk to them. Here we have made friends with a Swedish couple who have a small farm about three quarters of a mile away. They have been very kind giving us vegetables and fruit and books to read. You see no greengrocery is delivered out here. In return, though they would not take anything, Eric has dug potatoes and I have helped to pick them up. Eric is working at the other farm, it is not much money but they supply us with milk, some wood and some meat free.*

*I did miss Easter so much, it is not observed at all here, though I suppose it would be in the towns and maybe in the tiny church at Delamere if we could have got there. Eric was working all the time, and all day Saturday, but I made him say he wouldn't go on Sunday. We had bought Susan some pretty sugar eggs. She loved them and has made good headway with them too!*

*It has been very wet here for 8 days, today being the first nice day since we came back. This part is much damper than England, always Scotch mists in the offing, but beautiful on a really fine day.*

*From*

*Mollie, Eric and Susan.*

### *14th April 1950 – Delamere*

Tonight we have been gazing at Heaven. Eric's words – not mine. The weather has settled down to a dry spell with little or no wind, and the sky above is so beautiful. With Susan asleep in bed, Eric and I walk out behind the house into the clearing and stand in awe of the display above us.

It is like God has collected all the diamonds in the world and scattered them across a vast ocean in the sky. Such a huge number of them, impossible to count, sparkling with a vibrant intensity against shades of blue and black. Running across the centre is the straggling ribbon of the Milky Way, luminous and mysterious – with many more gemstones forming a dusty haze only Our Lord could have designed.

Eric points out the stars that make up Orion's belt, but we recognise nothing else. We still have no idea where to look to find the Southern Cross, yet I'm sure it is there.

On the ground stand the muted trees, and it seems to me they too are marvelling at the spectacle above their untidy heads. For the world around us is not completely silent. As Eric and I gaze in reverential respect at this divine display, there is a creaking and a whispering while the rooted multitude compares notes. Nature is smiling in appreciation of its own reflected glory.

### *16ᵗʰ April 1950 – Delamere*

It is a surprise to see such a strange-looking car turn into the drive in front of our house – especially when I see Eric in the passenger seat. The driver I don't know. I see white teeth in a dark face beneath a cloth cap, and then the vehicle comes to a stop and the engine dies. The front looks like an old-fashioned car with a huge bonnet hiding behind a pair of enormous headlamps, while the back half resembles something I would normally expect to see being pulled by a pony. I don't know what to make of it, but then Eric is standing in front of me, and the driver is approaching while doffing his cap. Instantly I am reminded of Hurtle's stories about abo's. Could this man be one?

'This is Bert, Mollie. Bert Joseph. He's working at Hooper's.'

It's in Eric's voice as soon as he speaks. A corner of my heart aches at that familiar sound of tightened, rasping breath. But I manage a smile and offer my hand to the man with a familiar name.

'Pleased to meet you, Mr Joseph.'

'G'day, Miss.'

He has a strong grip and the biceps to match. It is not long after noon on a warm autumn day, and I find myself distracted between concern for my husband's health and the amount of bare brown skin on show. The man is only wearing a vest and shorts – and no shoes. But then Eric

149

speaks again.

'Started with a cold. This morning. Think it's gone to my chest...'

'You've had an asthma attack.'

'Yes,' Eric nods. 'Seems like it. Joe asked Bert here to bring me home.'

I turn towards the man to offer thanks for helping my husband, but Eric has more to say.

'And there's something else... Bert has a young family and they're sleeping in the back of this thing while he does some temporary work at Joe's. It's called a Buckboard, by the way. That right?'

Bert Joseph nods with pride. 'Dodge Four. She's eighteen year old now.'

'So I was thinking,' Eric continues. 'We've got plenty of space. Could they stop here?'

It is typical of my husband's Christian values to want to help others he sees as being in need. I have to agree, and after looking all round the property Mr Joseph says he'd be very happy to take over our outhouses, if that is all right? I feel a slight relief that he shows no desire to take over our spare bedroom, but clearly anything will be a step up from their present accommodation. So while Eric puts his head under a towel for the benefit of a steam bath, Susan and I help our guest to tidy up outside. The next day I am introduced to Mrs Joseph and their nine year old son – appropriately named Sonny.


*6th May 1950 – Delamere*


I cannot believe it has been so long since I wrote in my journal. But since Bert and his family moved in with us there has been so much to think about, and even more to do. Whenever I have been about to pick up my pen, even to write to family in England, I have always been distracted by Susan, Eric, Mrs Joseph or Mrs Jacobson. On reflection, that is no bad thing. I do prefer to be busy, and I suppose I have now adapted to life here.

The weather has been pleasant, quite warm actually, while Eric has strangely suffered from several colds, and asthma never seems far away. If we were in Manchester I would have had him to the doctor's surgery on Stretford Road, but here all I can do is put my trust in patent bottled stuff I buy over the counter at the Delamere store – and that is something I have to rely on others to help with by providing transport.

On a better note, Eric has still been able to work so money continues to come in, and we do feel fortunate with the friends we have made. Susan has had Sonny as a playmate for three weeks now, although I have had to ask his mother to calm him down on the odd occasion. The frogs in our water tank are still there, but now they are a source of interest for a small boy with a fishing net. I wonder if boys are the same the world over? His attendance at school also seems a little erratic.

Tonight was probably one of our most unusual excursions. A cinema trip to the seaside! Eric has been feeling rough for a while now, and Bert suggested some sea air might help. Rapid Bay is a little over half an hour's drive from here, and it is the nearest place with a picture house. Both families pile into the Joseph family's car-lorry – Eric and I with the children sitting on the bench seats behind, and hanging on for dear life as Bert steers us along a narrow track towards the coast in the north.

Sonny Joseph takes it all in his stride as nine year old boys tend to do. Susan is nearly four, and is determined to match his independence, so she is not happy for Eric to hold her tightly on the way out. There are several little protests at first, but after ending up twice on her bottom when we meet a couple of potholes, she is a little more contrite. Sonny still sniggers at her discomfort, and I feel happier when Susan keeps her distance from him.

I am surprised to see houses close to the bay when we arrive. Bert tells us they belong to the families of quarry workers, and that the hut where we are to watch the film is a sort of community hall. He also tells me the fishing is particularly good here, and points out a half mile long pier over to our left that he tells us is where he sometimes joins the locals. Ships regularly moor at the far end to load up with limestone from the quarry, which sits out of our view within the cliff face. As we take our places in the cinema hut I feel an urge to whisper in Eric's ear.

'He's a fisherman. Did you know?'

'Yes. Comes here quite often, I believe.'

'I could die for a fish supper! See what you can do!'

The film is *Africa Screams*, starring Bud Abbott and Lou Costello. It is quite funny, and Eric laughs loudly the whole way through. They are a favourite of his, while I prefer Laurel and Hardy. The Joseph's smile a lot, although I don't think they understand many of the American gags. But everyone enjoys the antics of the smaller gorilla, even Susan, who tends to hide behind her fingers at anything remotely scary. Thankfully she doesn't seem to notice there is no ice cream on offer.

Bert Joseph with Sonny on Hooper's truck

*Delamere*
*Sunday 7/5/50*

*My dear Elsie and Alan,*

*Thanks very much Elsie for two letters, April 13th and 20th.*

*A wild rather bleak night tonight, with the wind howling round our little house. The weather has been lovely for the past month with some very warm days, but not too hot. We are told it is an exceptionally warm dry autumn, but at any moment the heavens may open and it can rain for weeks when these parts are just bogged up. However, we still have plenty of water in our tank (also plenty of frogs) so hope it will keep off a bit longer.*

*Eric is working at a wood mill about one and a half miles away, it is heavy work but regular hours, 5 day week, and he is much happier than at the shop.*

*Am busy trying to knit a cardigan for myself, they are so expensive. Anything woollen is a terrific price. How does it compare in England? According to the C&A adverts in the Daily Mirror, prices don't seem to have altered a great deal.*

*Did you see Joan? I kept reckoning the hours back – nine and a half and guessing what you might be doing.*

*Hope you are having some luck with a house.*

*The Swedish people are not new settlers. They have been here about 23 years. They are extremely nice people but Communists, so beware, we keep off politics anyway.*

*Very much love to you both, from*

*Mollie, Eric and Susan.*

Polishing day – one of my favourite pastimes. Some might find it odd that I can enjoy the labour involved, especially in the Australian climate; but for me it is a labour of love. My tin of beeswax has lasted well, and I take pleasure in applying exactly the right amount on my cloth before pressing with my fingers along the grain of the oak. It is a routine as simple and therapeutic as my nightly prayers: bringing out the amber glow as I complete every part is like basking in one of Mother's smiles. I have no idea of the sideboard's actual age, but I imagine it has graced many a social occasion, even before she was born in 1882. I remember the linen and soap that always lived in one particular drawer, and the impressive tea service that had its home in the left hand cupboard. What would she say to the meagre items her daughter has placed there, in another world so far away? But now I am a mother myself, and my own daughter wants some attention.

'Mummy! Mummy!'

She runs in from the veranda at the same time as I hear the engine of a vehicle approaching.

'What is it, Susan?'

'Mrs Yarker Song's here!'

She is referring to Mrs Jacobson. The Swedish lady has tried to teach her how to pronounce it properly, yet Eric and I still use the English version. This is the first time our neighbour has not arrived on foot. As I go outside I am surprised to see both our Swedish friends stepping out of their car, and I find myself suppressing a smile at recent hints of a drink problem.

'Hi to you, *min lilla flicka!*' Mrs Jacobson stoops down and tickles Susan under the chin as she so often does. Both of them giggle. I smile my own greeting as Mr Jacobson opens the boot and drags out a large trunk.

'What's this?'

'It's nothing,' says Mrs Jacobson. 'Or perhaps it is something. What are you thinking, Susan?'

I lead the way inside and hold open the door as the farmer enters with his bulky load. He sets it down in front of the sideboard, right next to my cloths and beeswax.

'Not there, Peter! Can you not see she is busy at her work?'

'Oh don't worry!' I say. But her husband is already shrugging his shoulders and shifting the trunk nearer to the table. He smiles at me, winks at Susan and returns to his car – job done.

'What is this?' I repeat as I bend down to retrieve the tin and my polishing cloths.

Mrs Jacobson is already undoing the catches. 'We have a few things that belong to Kitty. Too small for her now, and not ready for any little ones yet, so we are thinking best for Susan while you are still with us.' I start to protest, but she continues. 'Winter will be upon us next and what have you got? Look!'

She holds up a child's pair of green rubber wellington boots. Susan's eyes light up at once. But there is more. Out of the trunk and onto our table come several woollen jumpers and cardigans, a little coat with a hood attached, and even items of underwear, all washed and neatly folded.

I feel so touched by this lady's generosity. We seem like close friends and yet our language, our politics and even our religious beliefs are far apart. It is a genuine comfort for me to have another woman to speak to – especially one with such a compassionate nature.

We share a coffee that afternoon while Susan tries on some of her new clothes – especially the wellingtons. Mrs Jacobson admires Mother's sideboard, telling me she has nothing left at all from her own parents, apart from a wedding ring. She asks after Eric, and I feel I have to be honest and tell her my fears.

'He's gone to see a doctor in Yankalilla.'

'Why?'

'Well he has a problem with his elbow.' Instinctively I touch my own in the same spot Eric has shown me. 'It's very painful and swollen. He must have knocked it at Hooper's but he swears he hasn't. Or at least he doesn't remember. Anyway it's really bothering him and he's been off since Wednesday morning because he just cannot use it to work.'

'Oh my word! So he is not earning. That must be a worry for you.'

'Yes indeed. Mr Hooper has been very good though. Kevin had a delivery in Yankalilla today so he has taken Eric with him to see the doctor there. I said to ask him about his asthma too.'

Mrs Jacobson rolls her eyes. 'Hah! That doctor will know nothing about asthma. I don't like him. He is a *bedragare...* a man who tells false things? He tells me once I have collapsed because my muscles are too weak. You know what it was? You know what another man tell me at the hospital? That the pressure in my blood is not strong. Not my muscles! So I have little pills to make my blood stronger.'

'So you went to a hospital? The one in Victor Harbor?'

She nods. '*Ja.* It is a good hospital, but a long way from here. You tell your Eric not to listen to the Yankalilla man. I forget his name. He is not good. How is your family in England? Are they looking forward to your return?'

'Oh yes! Elsie and Alan can't wait to see how much Susan has grown. That reminds me – I have another magazine for you. Joan sent me one last month and I think Elsie will be sending another soon. Oh, and another bit of good news in the post today – even Eric doesn't know yet – our ship will pick us up at Adelaide after all!'

'Is that not what you arranged?'

'No!' I say as I retrieve a copy of *Woman's Weekly* from the sideboard drawer. 'We were told we would have to travel to Melbourne as the ship sailed from there straight to Fremantle. So I don't know what happened but I'm ever so glad. Eric was worried about having to go all that way. I think he said it would mean a whole day to get there?'

'At least! Not to mention so much extra expense. My word, Mrs Veale – maybe your God has smiled on you today, *ja?*'

It seems an odd thing for her to say. But while I am still worried about Eric's health, I look at my friend's smiling face and then at my over-dressed daughter in her coat and wellingtons – and feel it is indeed a good time to send a little prayer of thanks for looking after us all.

*Delamere S.A. 15/5/50*

*Dear Elsie and Alan,*

*Thanks very much for your letter of the 2nd. I shall look forward to the 'Woman's Own' Elsie, nobody else sends them, and when you send some more, could you include an 'Evening News' so we can get some idea from the adverts re houses, furniture etc? Susan will be thrilled with the colour books, just what she loves. Please don't bother about any other present, those will be ideal.*

*It has been lovely weather for the last 6 weeks, the driest autumn for 30 years. It was bad over the weekend, but lovely today though very cold, that suits me of course!*

*Am sorry to say Eric is off work due to his elbow. It has been swollen up for over a week, it seems like fluid. He got into Yankalilla to see the doctor, who wasn't much good, then tried Victor Harbour 35 miles away, Hurtle took him. The doctor there told him to poultice and gave him tablets, and if it doesn't disappear he will have to go to the hospital at Victor. I don't suppose he will be away long, and the Swedish lady has told me to go there if I want to, but would rather stay here if it's only a few days. Hurtle and family live in Yankalilla now 19 miles away, Grace expects her baby the first week in June.*

*Did I tell you we have a woodcutter, wife and*

*child camping here? They are away at the moment, but expect them back this week sometime. It makes it a little less lonely.*

*There is an egg famine round here just now. How about you and how much are they now? The last we got were 3/6 lb. But we can get plenty of dripping, very little lard and margarine.*

*Susan has just acquired a pair of Wellingtons and practically lives in them, she is so proud.*

*Just received word our ship will call at Adelaide after all so that will be much better.*

*No, Susan has not forgotten you both, on the contrary, she often talks about you, also her toy cupboard at Chorlton!*

*Much love from all three*

*Mollie*

### 22ⁿᵈ May 1950 – Delamere

Eric's birthday – and he is at home, thank heavens. Home from the hospital, that is. He went to Victor Harbor last Thursday, knowing he could be in overnight, but they kept him there over the whole weekend and wouldn't let him home until today. Of course he is quite cheery about it, but it has been worrying me sick. I kept thinking he must have got worse, but then on Saturday Hurtle got word through to Joe Hooper, who sent a message back with Bert Joseph. It's on occasions like this that I do wish we weren't so isolated.

Susan seems to accept everything as normal, and I sometimes envy her youth and innocence. But she must have missed her daddy as she gave the most enormous squeal when he walked through the door this morning. Naturally she had made him a *very* special birthday card, and I felt tears on my cheeks as I sat looking at my husband with Susan on his lap, happily pointing out all the flowers and animals she had drawn for him.

She will have her fourth birthday soon, and we are planning a little party for her, inviting the Jacobson's and the Joseph family to join in. Time seems to be playing tricks on me. I think back over Susan's short life so far – a time when Australia has dominated so much of my thoughts – and I can't believe how quickly those few short years have passed. Once I had imagined our little family living in a rich new world where the sun shone and we had plenty of everything, perhaps even a baby brother or sister too. As I write this the wind is howling outside, there is a scattering of raindrops and I suspect much more to follow. This world we live in seems very far from my dreams. At least we should be back in England at the right time, ready to get Susan into school – but who knows where?

We have taught her to write a little, and she seems to have a good memory for songs and hymns. Each night she says her little prayer, kneeling by her bed with hands clasped together:

'Gentle Jesus, Meek and Mild, Look upon this Little Child. Pity my simplicity, and teach me Lord to come to thee. God Bless Mummy and Daddy, Dandy and Sandy, Mr and Mrs Yarker Song, Auntie Elsie and Uncle Alan and Auntie Joan.'

*Delamere S.A.*
*24/5/50*

*My dear Elsie,*

*Very many happy returns! Are we too early or too late, I wonder? Whichever it is, lots and lots of love and best wishes. We wanted to send you a pair of nylons, but decided to bring them home with us as there is always a risk sending them through the post. Of course the Customs may think me a suspicious looking character when we land, but can pass them off as my own property then.*

*Thanks very much for your letter and one from Alan, both received yesterday. I hope all our letters have turned up by now as I have written pretty regularly, but it looks as if one may have got lost.*

*We have been having very heavy rain since last night, and howling winds. Glad to say Eric is home again and his elbow seems to be healing nicely, though I keep on poulticing. He has to ring the doctor this week-end to see if he can return to work.*

*Susan has a craze for dressing up at the moment, especially for long skirts so she can dance round and make them flare out. The Swedish lady at the farm gave her an old white silk frock, red sash and battered straw hat, she looks so comical in them but of course it's very serious and we keep straight faces! She is always talking of London, you and Alan, the things she is going to have and do when she gets to England. We told her about the books on the way, so every so often she enquires* "Is the boat coming. Has it got my books?"

*Last Sunday our woodcutter friends took us to a small place on the coast to do some fishing. We licked our lips thinking of fresh fish for tea (only had it 4 times since we landed). However, only one small fish consented to be caught, so we came home to the usual bread and cheese. Food is a real problem here, and eggs have been unobtainable for weeks. It would be alright in the city of course.*

*We were glad to read about the points system ending, and the sale of cream. Won't Joan have a good time in Devon? The cream ban has just been lifted here too, yesterday, and it is hinted butter may come off the ration but will go up in price. It is 2/2½ lb already.*

*Eric says he is going to write too so look out for his letter.*

*Much love to you both and a very happy birthday Elsie.*

*Mollie*

Outside the veranda

*3rd June 1950 – Delamere*

It has been quite a day. Susan's fourth birthday – and one I will never forget! We planned one or two surprises for her, but in the end it is Eric and I who received the biggest surprise.

The weather has been kind to us. At least it is dry enough to set up a trestle table outside. The Jacobson's come over early and help with everything, a bed sheet serving as a tablecloth and our shared collection of crockery making enough place settings for twelve. Kevin and Joan Hooper join us with their four year old daughter Kerry, and little Robbie who is about eighteen months old. We are all wrapped up against the cold and Susan has her wellington boots on as usual, but she is happily running around with the other children when we hear a lorry coming down the lane.

'Who's this, then?' says Eric. 'Well, who'd have thought it! That's Hurtle's old Bedford. Better crack open some more tinnies, Mollie. He's usually thirsty!'

I am surprised. We hadn't invited him and Grace as we know they are expecting baby number three at any moment. Perhaps there have been complications? Or more likely he has brought the money he owes Eric in back pay. That will be very welcome! I extract myself from a conversation about eggs with Joan Hooper and go with Eric to meet Hurtle as he trudges up the driveway. It is obvious from his face he hasn't expected to find so many of us here, and he hesitates not far from the entrance.

'Is Grace all right?' I say as we approach.

'What? Oh, yeah. She's whingeing a bit, mind. But nothing new there, eh? What's all this, then?' He swept an arm in the direction of our little gathering by the drying area.

'Susan's birthday!' says Eric. 'Good to see you, mate. We've got some beers. Come and join us!'

'Oh. Right.' His eyes avoid mine. 'Probably not a good idea, Eric. I wasn't going to stop anyways. Just had to give you this.' He pulls out an envelope from his pocket and pushes it forward.

'What is it?' As Eric reaches out to take it I sense the atmosphere change. There hasn't been any sun all day, but at that moment it feels like the clouds have got a lot thicker, and the temperature seems to plunge. I mutter some sort of excuse about needing to supervise the children, and turn away to let the men talk in private. But as I join Mr Jacobson and Kevin Hooper on the veranda I hear Eric's voice, raised in astonishment.

'A bill? You're joking! You're supposed to be paying ME!'

'Would either of you like some more beer?' I try to shut my ears to the heated conversation that is beginning just twenty feet away. But our neighbours are showing more interest in the scene over my shoulder.

'FORTY THREE QUID?'

Eric's voice is getting louder, and the conversation more aggressive. I turn to see both men squaring up for a fight. My neighbours clearly think the same, and as I glance to my left Mr Jacobson puts his drink back on the table and takes a pace or two nearer the argument.

The children's voices are stilled as the other women gather them up and head inside. Kevin joins Mr Jacobson in an attempt to calm the atmosphere on our driveway just as I see Eric being pushed backward by Hurtle. He lashes out with his fist as the other men reach him. I don't think Hurtle is hit, but he is angry, and I am stunned to see my husband lose his temper. I remind myself he had been a soldier, and was probably involved in far more serious bouts of violence in Palestine. I don't recall any more words – but I will remember forever seeing those four men embattled, two of them prepared to hurt each other before one slinks off back to his truck, and the other stands his ground. I can see the redness of his skin at the back of Eric's neck, anger seeping through every pore. The envelope and Hurtle's bill lie on the ground at his feet. I am so hollow inside, watching our world fall apart yet again.

*Delamere*
*South Australia*
*6th June 1950*

*My Dear Elsie and Alan,*

*Thank you for your letter dated May 15, which arrived on the 24th, and thank you for your good wishes. I'm sorry I'm a bit late in writing you in time for your birthday Elsie still I did think of you last Sunday.*

*Well now prepare yourselves for a bad shock. Hurtle has at last shown himself up in his true colours. He's put this place on the market, and has prepared a bill for me which he delivered on Sue's birthday. He's told us in fact, we have to get out, and has charged me £5 a week board for the time we stayed with him and Grace. £3 a week for rent and meat while we lived in two rooms behind the shop, over £40 for the removal from Keith to Delamere, and 25/- a week for the rent of this place. This he claims with the £5 a week he has paid me while I was at Keith, comes to a wage of £11 odd a week, and the award wage is £8 odd. So he reckons he owes me nothing, and I worked 70 to 90 hours a week while at Keith, which with overtime should bring my wage to over £16 a week, and to charge me those fabulous prices for rent and removal, well I was staggered.*

*I've had a first class row with him, and now we are looking for a place in Glenelg or Adelaide for the next few weeks, so I suppose we shall be moving again soon. Hurtle is supposed to be a Mason, and their vow is to take no reward against the innocent and he professed himself a brother in Christ. Well, well we live and learn, and I have learnt my lesson, and I shall be careful who I trust in future.*

*Mollie is well and so is Susan. She had a party last Saturday.*

*We've written to find out if there are any cancellations on earlier boats, but don't hope too much. Lots of love from all three of us. See you at least we hope in September.*

*Yours with love,*

*Eric*

*9ᵗʰ June 1950 – Delamere*

Mrs Jacobson stands facing me in our living room, her eyes rimmed red, matching my own. It is not yet time to say goodbye, but both of us know our lives will never be the same again.

'I promise you it will be looked after.'

She gives a slight nod to emphasise her words, and I know she is sincere. We have known each other barely three months, but it seems like three years. This Swedish lady has given me more support in a foreign land than anyone, and it is a comfort to me to know Mother's sideboard will still receive love and care that matches my own. Well – almost.

'Perhaps... once you are more settled, it will be possible to have it shipped back to you in England?'

I shake my head. 'No. It is a nice thought, but somehow I think we will have other demands on our money. We have to start again from scratch, Eric will have to find work, we don't know what the housing situation will be, so...'

'I understand. But you will succeed. You have the strong spirit, like your daughter?'

That makes me smile a little. Susan's tenacity for life come-what-may is indeed a source of strength. She has been told we are moving again, and she has just accepted it. So long as she has her toys and her colouring books (and mummy and daddy) then her world is complete.

Eric and I talked long into the night after his row with Hurtle, and this last week we have also spent a good many hours in conversation with the Jacobson's and the Hooper's. Bert and his family left straight after the party. We have been given two week's notice to quit by Hurtle, but Eric wants us to be gone as soon as possible, so tomorrow will be our last day here before we move to Adelaide. Thankfully our friends have found us a small flat in Glenelg that we can rent until we sail for England.

But we have to leave so much behind. With one exception it is not so much the physical things we have accumulated. Our lives in Delamere have been enriched by the people we met, and we will leave this part of Australia with heavy hearts. My own sadness is compounded by a more personal loss, and I have to tell myself it is my way of giving thanks for all the generous help we have been given.

I had closed my mind to the possibility that the sideboard might cost too much for us to ship home. Somehow I was determined we would be able to save enough money, but with Eric losing out on wages while off work with his elbow, and then Hurtle's bill, the sums just do not add up. Even now we are relying on favours sprung from a brief friendship to find lodgings, and to transport us there.

'You know I will visit you at Glenelg? We will be all girls together, with Kitty, and have an afternoon tea?'

I smile properly this time. 'Thank you. I'd like that. It sounds very English!'

'*Ja.* But when you get back to England, don't forget how I showed you to make a proper Swedish coffee!'

Mrs Jacobson reaches into her apron pocket and produces two precious objects like a magician pulling a rabbit from a hat.

'Eggs! Where on earth did you get them? I know there haven't been any for weeks at the store.'

She smiles. 'Ah-ha. That would be telling. Now what about that coffee?'

'Why not? I'll fill up the kettle. Would you like one frog or two?'

# Part Four

## *Glenelg*

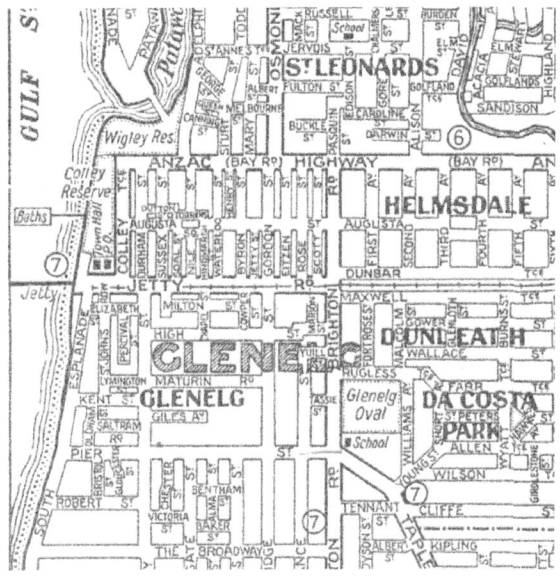

*22 Byron St, Glenelg*
*12th June 1950*

*Dear Elsie and Alan,*

*I expect you will be wondering where we have managed to end up! Fortunately, the people Eric worked for at the mill were kind and helpful. They live in rough sheds and tents in the woods at Delamere, but have this flat in an Adelaide suburb as a permanent home. They tried to find somewhere else here for us, but no use, so have let us come in here as it is only for 10 weeks. You see we had to have a furnished place as we had very little furniture, the beds etc being Hurtle's.*

*We came yesterday afternoon, today has been a public holiday in honour of the King's Birthday, so we have been out all day. Tomorrow Eric will see what kind of job he can get until August 24th.*

*It is difficult to explain in letters just what occurred with Hurtle. He is not, however, the genuine person we thought. I think it is spite because we do not like this country sufficiently to stay. But he doesn't realise that it is mostly due to him that things were so difficult. However, hope we can explain it properly to you one day, but I would never have believed that he wouldn't pay Eric any more than the £5 per week he got. 70 to 90 hours a week for £5. He says he has paid the equivalent of £11 by making up a big bill against us for rent etc, and keep. £5 a week whilst we lived at his house. As you know we had to sleep out at his sister's, I used my own bed linen, did a lot of work and bought some food etc. Anyway, we have finished with him now. I do not blame Eric because I too thought Hurtle was OK.*

*We are quite close to the sea here, plenty of shops, constant hot water and a wireless! Until we can get some wood we have only a small electric fire, so it is a little chilly as just now we are having some quite cold days. In Adelaide itself, however, it keeps very temperate during the winter. We went this afternoon and had to shed the cardigan under my coat. We went to the Koala Bears Farm – Susan enjoyed herself thoroughly, but mostly on the chutes, rockers etc.*

*In all the rush and excitement I almost forgot to thank you for the lovely little books for Susan, also the mags for me, which arrived all together last Wednesday. Susan got busy straightaway, her first painting efforts and she didn't do too badly. She had a little birthday party and cake with 4 candles –* "fires all round" *she calls them, which she enjoyed blowing out so much, Eric had to relight them about 6 times!*

*Love to your Mother and sisters Elsie, and lots of love to you both from all of us.*

*Mollie*


*12ᵗʰ June 1950 – Glenelg*

We are in a different world, living in a normal house on a normal street. I have a proper kitchen all to myself and a key to our front door. But even this artificial reality scarcely resembles the dream we had for ourselves twelve months ago. It is a game of "let's pretend" as we face the next few weeks adjusting once again to some kind of routine. Eric and I are still in shock to find ourselves here, essentially now living out of our suitcases, and under pressure to find enough money to afford our passage home.

Tomorrow will be a long one for Eric, as he looks for

whatever he can find to provide the funds we so desperately need. There are only eight weeks left before we must pay the balance for our passage home, and so he needs wages worth at least £5 a week again. But I have never seen him so determined. His scrap with Hurtle seems to have fired him with a positive energy that almost exhausts me. Physically I have struggled to keep up with him today. Twice he had to apologise as he went striding on with Susan, leaving me behind like an afterthought. While I have been feeling tired and slightly nauseous, Eric is just the opposite and has a ravenous appetite. At least my first attempt at an egg custard (with real eggs) went down well. I couldn't face it myself.

So now my daughter and husband are both in bed, and despite my tiredness I cannot yet find sleep. Their breathing is so different. Eric is flat on his back, rhythmically snoring through every second intake of breath. Susan lies on her side, lips pursed together as she emits an occasional little whistle. I marvel at them both, untroubled in their dreams while to me the world still seems a vast and worrying place.

*14th June 1950 – Glenelg*

'Success!'

Eric is beaming broadly when he enters at the same time as a strong gust of wind. The draught from the door immediately extinguishes the small flame I have managed to coax from under the logs in our fire grate. It has taken me over half an hour to get this far, and so my facial reaction is probably not what my husband expected.

'I got the job! Starting tomorrow... What?'

'Splendid. You've got another one now. See if you can get a fire going, Eric. I'm all out of puff.' I am on my knees and feel a little giddy as I stand up again. 'Sorry love. Still a bit queasy. So go on. What did they say?'

Eric bends down to look at the pile of logs I made up while he was out. 'You've too much on here, Mollie. Start with a few less, eh?' He takes off a couple of the bigger pieces and pokes the remainder around before reaching for more paper and matches. 'Yes, nice lady. Her name's Win, and like that fellow yesterday said, she needs an extra pair of hands, especially early in the mornings. Is this the only paper we have?'

I join Susan at the table, busy as usual with her colouring books, and pass another sheet of newspaper to Eric before sitting down heavily.

'Hmm. I wanted to keep that article about Korea. Looks like things are getting worse there. Never mind – where was I?' He starts to roll the sheet diagonally across until he has a kind of paper pole about two foot in length. Then he presses it flat on the floor.

'Early mornings?'

'Yes. From about half past five.' Eric folds the flattened newspaper pole into a 'V' shape, and then continues to fold end over end until he has a kind of plait about nine inches in length. 'That's the time someone has to be there to open up for fishing bait. Sometimes to get wood deliveries too. Do you think these might be damp?'

'I don't know. You're the expert.' I watch as Eric feeds his simple firelighter under the partly burned logs I started with this morning. 'What about the money?'

'Ah! That's the best bit. She pays between five and seven pounds a week depending on how many early mornings I can do. And I'll do all of them! There – that should do it!'

We watch a tiny flame grow in strength as it works its way beneath the logs and starts to curl tightly around an inviting ember. I shiver, partly from being cold and partly in anticipation of being warm again. But it is certainly good news that Eric can soon start earning, and I tell him so.

He smiles in acknowledgement, then turns back to the

grate. 'Looks more like it. Let's see if we can help the flame a bit more. Another piece?'

I hand him one more sheet of newspaper as he retrieves the shovel from the log basket.

'You're quiet, Suey? Are you all right?' He looks over his shoulder while he moves to balance the shovel upright on the lip of the grate, resting the handle against the bottom edge of the mantle above.

Susan looks up from her work, screwing her eyes tight shut and shakes her head.

'She says she's got a tummy ache now,' I say. 'Ate all her breakfast though, so I just think she's coming out in sympathy!'

Eric laughs as he leaves the shovel to mask the smouldering fire behind and picks up the open sheet of newspaper to hold against it. 'Hah! Typical female. Want to see Daddy do a trick, Sue? You can be my assistant if you like.'

Susan looks up with interest. 'What are you doing, Daddy?'

'I'm drawing the fire. Although not in the way you might draw something. See – by blocking off the air *above* the flames I'm making the air pass *under* them. That draws the heat into the wood and makes the fire burn better. Can you see the orange flame behind the paper?'

Susan climbs out of her chair and nervously peers past where her father is knelt covering the open grate with the newspaper.

'Don't worry! The shovel protects it. It's only a small flame, but we want it to get bigger. So why don't you open the door a little and we'll give it a bit of a nudge?'

I'm not so keen on that idea, but Susan is more enthusiastic. She runs over to the door and throws it open as wide as she can.

'Eric!' I cry out in alarm as the rush of air from the open doorway instantly achieves its purpose. The newspaper bursts into flame and I am impressed with the speed at which my husband moves. He flings the offending article onto the hearth and stamps on it, sending tiny wisps of blackened newsprint tinged with red spinning into the air.

'Shut the door Susan!' we yell in unison. And she does – loudly. Then:

'That was a good trick, Daddy! Do it again!'

### 21$^{st}$ June 1950 – Glenelg

A week later and we have fallen into some kind of routine. Eric is settling in to his new job at Win's Emporium, and has had no further accidents with the fire. I must admit that is probably because the weather has been much warmer so we haven't needed it. Susan and I have had a good look around town, and we even managed to attend church on Sunday as there is a lovely Congregational church quite close to us on Jetty Road. (Eric works nearby opposite the tram terminus.)

My stomach has gone back to normal, thank goodness, and my appetite is much better. We even get to eat together early evening as Eric finishes work at four o'clock. Susan keeps wanting to call at Win's to see her Daddy behind the counter. She loves it in there as the shop sells all sorts of ironmongery and household items as well as fishing tackle and bait. There is always a strong whiff of paraffin and other smells that she somehow finds very appealing, and it is a handy place to call at on the way to or from the beach.

For that has been a regular part of our days in Glenelg. I feel a need to get out of this flat as much as I can. It belongs to Joe Hooper and I even feel nervous about using his crockery. I stripped the sheets as soon as we arrived and replaced them with our own, but I can never get away from the thought that we are living in someone else's pocket. So while the weather encourages us to venture out I am happy to do so. I have always been drawn to the sea, and as I sit watching Susan playing in the sand with her new bucket and spade I find my eyes drawn to distant horizons. The prospect of another war is not so far away, and if that should happen Eric has said it could play havoc with the shipping. It feels almost selfish for me to wish for another conflict to be avoided, just so our little family can find its way home, and yet I can't help myself. I see an occasional ship pass by and my thoughts wander to that fragile thread connecting me to my family so far away.

On the beach at Glenelg

*22 Byron St, Glenelg,*
*28ᵗʰ June/50*

*Dear Elsie and Alan,*

*Thanks very much Elsie for your letter of the 8th. Now I wonder how you went on last Saturday. We were thinking of you, do hope all went well and according to plan. Dear old Zion. How I wish I could trip up those steps. We were ever so glad to hear the target had been more than passed! You must all have worked jolly hard.*

*Now we are wondering if we shall get home as planned, this dreadful news about Korea may lead to anything. It's strange but for a while I felt it would be unwise to look forward too much, but what will happen if we can't I don't know. Anyway it's no use wondering, we shall have to await developments.*

*Susan is almost a full time artist. Those books you sent started her off, then I got some "Magic" Painting Books, and as those were finished in a couple of days, got a real paint box. That was on Monday, today Wednesday, several of the colours are more than half gone. She is very serious about it.*

*Today we have been watching a rough sea, Susan's first. She wouldn't let me go near as* "we might get drowned". *The beautiful weather broke last Saturday – a lot of heavy rain since and wind but it has never been very cold yet. The floods in N.S.W. are dreadful, and we are worried about some friends we made on the ship who are living in the flooded areas. They too are going back to England but have a home to sell, and were doing it up to get a good price, so hope it isn't damaged.*

*Mr Hunter is a "dark horse", it's the first I've heard about him being engaged.*

*Susan and I went to the Winter Sales the other day. Of course we didn't get anything much, we were much too late for any bargains, but Sue had a good time on escalators and lifts and demanded a cup of tea in a café so we visited the cafeteria. She loves looking at pretty things and not without some requests of course!*

*God bless you both and please pray that we might*

*be allowed to come home, won't you.*
*Lots of love,*

*Mollie*

*3rd July 1950 – Glenelg*

Eric is in bed and I am back at my table writing again. It is a nuisance but I feel bloated and too uncomfortable for sleep. So many things are passing through my mind just now, hopes as well as fears. There has been a reason for my physical discomfort lately but I have been too scared I might jinx something by writing anything down. I keep thinking back to Delamere and Mother's sideboard, alone and unloved. I want to be able to touch it once more, to see the amber glow beneath my fingers and to feel Mother's energy pass through me. I'm lonely again, and a little frightened. I don't want to wake Eric.

*Friday July 7th*

*Dear Elsie and Alan,*

*Please excuse pencil. I was about to write you early this week with the news that we were expecting the family to increase next January. However, it is not to be. Late on Monday a threatened miscarriage started, the doctor kept me in bed all Tuesday and Wednesday in an effort to avert it, but 11 o'clock Wednesday night had to be rushed in this hospital in Glenelg. (What a blessing we had left Delamere.)*
*I had an operation early yesterday and feel much better now. Hope I can get out soon as Eric has had to stop off work to look after Susan as we don't know*

179

*a soul here.*

*Haven't the slightest idea what caused it, and feel so foolish as I had no trouble when Susan was on the way.*

*Thank you so much Alan for your letter, shall have to answer that when I get home.*

*Please excuse more now, only I did want to write you myself.*

*All my love to you both,*

*Mollie*

*15ᵗʰ July 1950 – Glenelg*

Life is so fragile, tragic and wonderful. I am back in our little flat and I am so full of emotions. On the one hand I feel desperately sad to have lost that little speck of life that had started inside me. It was just not the right time. On the other hand I have been overwhelmed with the show of love from Eric and others. Susan was very sweet when I was ill. The first day I had to stay in bed she brought me her teddy and stuck it in beside me for company when she went out. Constant enquiries as to whether I was better yet, and when I came home she cuddled up close to me and fell asleep, not wanting to leave me for an instant.

Then there is the more practical worry about the financial situation – again. We now have a bill to pay for both the doctor and the stay in hospital. If we had been living nearer to the Royal Adelaide it would have been easier, but I had to go to the nearest private hospital because there simply wasn't time. I had begun to haemorrhage and the doctor was doing his best to save my baby. Then it was too late. They wouldn't let me out for six days, so that's six lots of money going out that we hadn't accounted for – and six with no money coming in either, as Eric had to look after Sue. Oh dear! What a mess. Thankfully Win has offered Eric overtime. The poor love hates to leave my side after this, but we both have to put on a happy face for Susan. There is no way Eric can afford to stay at home any longer.

### *16ᵗʰ July 1950 – Glenelg*

A strange sound is coming from Susan's room. Her young voice is shouting about baking a cake accompanied by what sounds like a tin tray being battered into a different shape.

'Susan! Stop that horrid noise!'

There is silence for a moment. 'I'm not being noisy. I'm singing!' Then she starts again: 'How d'ya do. How d'ya do. How d'ya do!'

'Susan! That sounds positively awful. Please stop it at once. I've got a letter for you from Mrs Jacobson.'

'For me?' She stands in the doorway, holding a wooden spoon that has probably been serving as a drumstick.

I hold up the little sheets of blue paper that were inserted into the envelope containing my own letter. 'Look! She's drawn you some pictures too. There's Dandy and Sandy, and look – I think this is one of the lambs.'

'Ahh... What's its name?'

'I don't know. Shall I read it to you?' Susan drops the spoon-stick and eagerly scrambles onto the chair next to me. She knows she can't yet sit on my lap because Mummy is still not well enough. Then I begin to read:

'Dear Susan, Dandy and Sandy sends their love to you. Last week they had a lovely breakfast. When I said "Hello" to them in the morning they looked very hungry and sad, just like this.'

Susan giggles at the pen picture of two cats with enormous tails and whiskers, sat together like bookends, each with a forlorn expression.

Then I continue: 'So I said "Never mind pussy-boys, I have something for you," and they looked quite happy again, like this.' Susan roars with laughter at two similar shapes, now with very broad smiles.

'She's given them a mouse!' She is quite right, as just underneath the cat drawing is another that resembles something with a long thin tale. Mrs Jacobson goes on to say the mouse has fallen into the cream, and so the combination has made a fabulous feast for those two hungry cats. It may have been a made-up story for my daughter's benefit, or it may very well have been true, but the thought of that little household and its familiar occupants cheers up Susan and I at a time when we very much need it.

'So what do you think?'

Susan has gone to bed, and Eric and I are sat at the table. On it is Eric's diary, a notebook and pencil, and a large envelope stuffed with paper money. I have counted and re-counted it, and Eric has been writing everything down, adding up columns and making adjustments as he consults his diary.

I try again. 'How bad is it?'

Eric still says nothing for a moment, keeping his focus on the scribbled figures, and then glancing back at his diary. 'It's not *bad*. It's just... tight. I think we'll be okay to raise the balance in time, but I'll just have to ask Win if she wouldn't mind paying me three days in advance that week. I think she'll be okay with it, though.'

'Eric, are you sure? Remember Mrs Jacobson still owes us some money.'

'Yes, but we'll need to draw on that after I've paid the balance. And I'll still have one last week at the Emporium with overtime thrown in. It has to be done, Mollie! We can't live off fresh air!

It feels awful living hand-to-mouth like this, but we have no choice. Eric sleeps like a log every night, exhausted from his working day, while I seem to take hours to find sleep. But I have to be strong for him, and to Susan and the outside world I must appear cheerful and full of confidence. It isn't easy.

*22 Byron St, Glenelg*
*18/7/50*

*Dear Elsie and Alan,*

    *Thanks very much for a letter from each of you. Alan's arrived today together with the copies of the "Evening News" (how good to see it again). Also Elsie, thanks very much for the second lot of "Woman's Own" sent on from Delamere. I'm glad the others will arrive soon. Have enjoyed them very much especially the story of the Princesses. I am passing them to the Swedish lady at Delamere.*

    *Well Elsie, I think you did marvellous at the Summer Effort, my, you must have worked jolly hard. Have just been reading the latest "Hand in Hand" which also arrived today, and am glad to see things seem to be improving all round for Zion. Wouldn't Mother and Father have been glad?*

    *I'm sorry I didn't tell you Eric was working, quite thought I had done, only writing so many letters I forget what I have said to different people.*

    *We are having beautiful weather. The winter is quite the nicest thing about Australia. On Sunday we took our lunch down to the beach. Susan paddled and had a great time.*

    *Well, the* Orcades *is on its way here from London, so all being well it won't be long now before we set sail once more! Poor Eric is having a bad time with his nose, and some asthma, am hoping the voyage will do him good.*

    *Much love to you both from*

*Mollie, Eric and Susan*

*5ᵗʰ August 1950 – Glenelg*

There are times when I thank God my husband knows how to handle a screwdriver – and also where to find one when the time calls. Bless her, Susan had our best interests at heart, but today she did send us into something of a panic. Eric had left work early for once and we ate dinner about five o'clock.

'Are you watching the time?'

'Goodness, Mollie! Nearly half past,' says Eric. 'Susan, leave your vegetables. We've got to run!'

'Why?'

'Our ship's coming! She'll be sailing right past any time now! Come on. We don't need to be out for long.' I pick up Susan's coat as well as my own and help her put it on. Normally one to do everything in a rush, today our daughter has turned into a slowcoach. Eric has grabbed his camera and is already opening the door as I don my jacket. Then Susan runs off into her bedroom.

'Suey! What are you doing?' cries Eric.

A muffled shout comes from the back of the flat. 'She's bringing her dolly,' I say in translation as I follow Eric down the path at the side of our building. As I reach the gate I hear Susan slam the fly-screen door behind her, and I hold out my hand for her to grab with her free one.

'Shouldn't we have locked up?' I say to Eric as we catch him up on the other side of the road.

'I suppose so. I'm not going back for the key now though. It'll be alright for a short while. *Orcades* isn't going to wait for us!'

So we head off to the beach, Susan for once protesting at the fast pace. I explain to her that Daddy read in the newspaper the other day that the ship we are due to sail on to England is expected to leave Port Adelaide just before half past five today, and we should see it quite clearly from our beach at Glenelg as it heads towards Melbourne to drop off another lot of migrants. Luckily for us our timing is perfect. A large ocean-going liner is already clear to see on our right, steaming east to pass Kangaroo Island. *Orcades* has sailed all the way from England, and in less than three weeks it will be back here at Adelaide to take us all back home.

RMS Orcades

Eric carefully focuses his camera at the distant vessel while Susan sits on the sand next to me, clutching her dolly and wondering what all the fuss is about. I find myself feeling quite emotional at this first glimpse of the ship that has been a part of my dreams for so long. Every last penny we have is being spent on it, and now the physical object is in front of me I have a tear running down my cheek.

'It doesn't look very big,' Susan observes.

Eric joins us, his face lit up in boyish excitement. 'Actually, it's a lot bigger than the one we came on, Suey! Supposed to be faster too.' He sits next to me and squeezes my hand while all three of us watch our all-important transport home gradually disappear from view. It only takes a few minutes, but we are all shivering with cold as we head back up Jetty Road, Eric waving to Win inside her shop as we pass the Emporium on our right. When we reach the door to our little flat it becomes clear we have a problem.

'It's locked.' Eric turns to me, eyebrows raised in silent question.

'Don't look at me,' I say. 'You're the one with the key.'

'But I haven't got it! I told you not to lock up...'

'No, you didn't! And I didn't lock it. Susan was the last one out. You didn't set the catch, did you, darling?'

Susan beams and nods. 'Like you showed me.' She is very proud of herself.

Eric does a perfect impression of Oliver Hardy, throwing his hands up in the air with a look of pained defeat on his face.

'Another fine mess?' I can't resist turning mimic. 'So what are we going to do now? Apart from throttling our daughter.'

Eric calms down rapidly. Then he rattles the fly-screen door and runs his fingers over the hinges. 'Wait here. I think I've got a great idea, Stanley.'

So Eric runs off to the Emporium to borrow a screwdriver, and after a few minutes work at the hinges we are soon back in the warmth. Laurel and Hardy might be good for providing the laughs in similar situations, but I prefer Eric's more practical solution to a problem we quickly see from the funny side.

*Tuesday, August 8th/50*

*Dear Elsie and Alan,*

*I am hoping this letter will reach you on or about the 16th, because it brings to you our most sincere good wishes for that happy anniversary. May you have many, many happy years together. And I want to tell you how very much Eric and myself have appreciated your ever ready help in the past, not to mention having to put up with us for a while in the future. I do hope that we can be of equal service to you if at any time you should need our help. Elsie has been much more than a sister-in-law to me and I shall always remember all she has done for me since mother died.*

*Thank you Alan for your letter of July 27th. If I close my eyes I can imagine just how the garden looks from your description. I'm glad the rose bush on the grave is blooming.*

*Yes, the 24th draws nearer. Eric has got the passport etc out tonight, ready to go to the Orient line office tomorrow.*

*It has been very cold (that is for Australia) today, but I sat on the beach yesterday whilst Susan played.*

*I am glad to hear that everything is OK at Sale Moor, as have not heard from Bert for some time.*

*Joan is looking forward to meeting us. The ship is scheduled to dock at Tilbury, so hope they don't alter it at the last minute. You know I cannot really believe we are coming home.*

*Some more mags came this morning Elsie, thank you very much, they are lovely. I have several to send you and must get them off tomorrow.*

*Our love as always,*

*Mollie*

*13th August 1950 – Glenelg*

I don't like to write again about our money situation, but I feel it is necessary to do so one final time. In the last few days it has dominated our conversations. To begin with, last Thursday Eric went into the city to pay the balance of our ticket home. It was right at the last minute, and it was such a relief to us both to know with absolute certainty that our passage is booked and paid for.

With less than two weeks to go, Susan and I have braved some squally showers just to get out of the flat and have something to do. I daren't get on a tram into the city in case I'm tempted to spend what little money we have left, while Eric (bless him) is still working until two days before we sail to earn as much as he can. Lord knows when he will next be in a position to bring home a wage packet.

But last Saturday Susan and I had a lovely surprise: a visit from Mrs Jacobson. She had promised to send me the balance of the money we had agreed for the sideboard, but instead she brought it in person.

'Here Susan,' beckons our Swedish friend. 'This envelope is for you, and this one is for your Momma. Go! Give both to her, yes?'

Susan is in shy mood, with her tongue wedged between her lips in a curious smile. She trots over to where I am sitting at the table and holds the envelopes out for me to take.

'Now Mrs Veale... No! I will use your proper name. Mollie, is it not? It has been too long to be so formal. Mollie, you will understand that both of these contain money. Peter and I are discussing much about the Veale family. We count our good fortune that our situation has not been as yours is. You have been unlucky, and it is not fair that you leave in dire straits, so we have upped our price a little. No! Do not speak. I have not finished. Your sideboard cannot have a price – I understand that. It is beyond price because of what it means to you. So for that reason I do not think it matters if what I pay is not as we said. Please – allow me to pay a little more. We are still friends, yes?'

I say goodbye to my friend Helga Jacobson for the last time a few minutes later. She refuses to stay longer, saying she has to meet her daughter Kitty in town. I hope that is true, as it is still a long journey from Delamere just to spend ten minutes in our company. But I think she knew, as I did, that emotions would run high – and getting tearful in front of Susan was something neither of us wanted.

Mother's sideboard is in good hands.

*Wednesday, 16/8/50*

*Dear Elsie and Alan,*

*Very many thanks for Elsie's letter of the 10th received this morning.*

*I'm sorry I did not mention that we were still hoping to sail on the 24th Aug. You see I thought you understood that we were coming then unless another war broke out which would probably upset all shipping arrangements. Yes, we hope to arrive in London on September 18th. Joan says she is going to meet us but didn't say she would be going to Manchester. She wants to know if she is to book us a room in London for one night, but of course, we shall not know until a few days before, at what time the ship will arrive. If it is late on the 18th we shall probably not disembark until the following morning. So we shall have to let both you and Joan know definitely as soon as we can.*

*If Joan is staying in London it would be nice to*

*have one day with her. I hardly think a bedroom will be necessary except for Susan as am sure we could talk all night!*

*Please Elsie, do not worry about our beds etc, or put yourselves to any inconvenience. It is extremely good of you to have us, and although I know how welcome we are, hope that we can soon have our own home again, though what we shall put in it I don't know! Shall have my eyes glued to the s/hand furniture adverts, judging by the way we couldn't get much for our furniture last year we ought to be able to find some at reasonable prices, I hope.*

*It is impossible to bring the sideboard home and we have just sold it to our Swedish friends. Am trying to get used to the idea of being without it, but it would have been too expensive, so we are bringing the crockery etc., which is all packed in tea chests and this will travel with us on the same ship.*

*In case you would like to send a line whilst we are en route, will give you the address, but if you are busy don't bother. You have been so good writing every week. The Orcades only calls at Colombo and Port Said so think I will give you the Port Said address. A letter should be addressed as follows:-*
*Mr & Mrs E J Veale*
*Tourist "B" Class Passengers to London*
*Orient Line RMS "Orcades"*
*C/o Messrs Wm. Stapledon & Sons*
*Port Said*
*The ship is due there on September 11th.*

*I will write again next week, but it maybe after we have sailed so will be posted from Fremantle on the 28th Aug.*

*Is it really true? Must ask Eric to pinch me!*

*Hope you have both had a happy anniversary today.*

*Lots of love from all three –*

*Mollie*

*26th August 1950 – On board "Orcades"*

There are barely three pages left in George Alcock's little notebook. But it is enough. Dear George – I did write and thank him for all his help, both practical and spiritual, but I never got a reply. Too late now, but I still think of him and his wife with their American car. I remember Marjorie being in tucks, laughing at Eric's Stanley Holloway monologue over a fish supper. I think of the smiles on people's faces. Our little family was welcomed by so many strangers, who quickly became friends. The climate has not been quite as friendly. This land of sunshine and promises has also been stormy and sadly disappointing. We have lots of memories, not all of them unhappy – and I feel my life has been enriched somehow by coming to Australia.

We sailed early yesterday morning. Lined up with other returning migrants we looked on as the coast gradually slid away – just as only ten months ago we watched its stealthy approach. We talked about Hurtle one more time, and so all three of us startled our fellow passengers by blowing a concerted raspberry in his honour. Again Eric and I have separate cabins on the lower deck – he sharing with two other men, while Susan and I get our own private cabin. How much older she seems than on our outward voyage! And yet she is still happy to scream and push alongside other children on something called "The Slippery Dip" in the nursery area.

What more to say? Well, I could mention the way in which the ship is rolling in rough seas. Perhaps that is only to be expected as Eric and I have got used to making heavy weather of things. Personally I have had enough of travelling. I don't want any more adventures in strange countries or climates. I want to sleep in a bed I can call my own. I want to collect my daughter from an English school in the afternoon. I want to walk with her to buy sweets and a copy of the *Manchester Evening News* from the shop on Barlow Moor Road. I *need* an ordinary life again.

But my extraordinary life of the last year has not been wasted. I've been to a pink part of the globe where people do more than throw strange sticks in a circle. Some of them have compassion and humility. Some have a generosity of spirit that puts me to shame, and who taught me so much about humanity. For that I feel I have paid a price I could not normally afford: part of me that was a part of Mother. Someone else's fingers will caress and admire that old sideboard in future; someone else will inherit new memories – so perhaps it was time to let go.

**PASSAGE TICKET TOURIST "B" CLASS**

OTN<u>O</u> 8364

The persons named hereon have secured a Tourist B Class passage (subject to the conditions on the covers and other pages of this ticket) from the port of

The Orient Line Steamship "...ORCADES..." of

Adelaide ............to the or about 28,000 ...tons register

port of ...................as Master's option, by the above-named Steamship, and have paid £E36/-/- stg. converted at 125% equals £A45/-/- on account of the full passage money of £E £158/10/- stg.

of the Twentyfourth day of August ...1950

NAMES OF PASSENGERS

On behalf of the Proprietors and the Managers of the Orient Line.
M. G. ANDERSON & CO. LIMITED Agents

MR. & MRS. E. J. VEALE
MISS S. VEALE

per ...........................

being a berth in a............. berth cabin.

Adelaide 17th May 19 50

| PASSAGE MONEY: | Converted | | Australian Equivalent | BRITH No. 778 Cabin 749/50 | No. of Persons | | | |
|---|---|---|---|---|---|---|---|---|
| £ English Stg. | @ % | | | | Full Fares | Half Fares | Qtr. Fares | Free |
| Deposit £ 36 : - : - | 125 £ | 45 : - : | | | 2 | 1 | - | - |
| Balance £ 122 10 : - | 125 £ | 153 : - 6 | | Balance payable not less than 10 days before embarkation | | | | |
| Total £ 158 10 : - | | £ 1082 6 | | Date Balance Signed Paid | | | | |

Cancelling Ticket No. 4307
by same voyage

1 0 AUG 1950

# Author's Note

Mollie's story is not unique. History tells us that many more adventurers returned to the UK after failing to make a home in Australia. But not many will have documented their story to such a degree.

What you have just read is a true story, and the letters I have reproduced are certainly authentic, while edited for content. But the journal itself is largely my own interpretation of my mother's experiences. This has been culled partly from the letters, and partly from personal anecdotes. There has also been a considerable amount of research undertaken, as I have been determined to make Mollie's story as accurate as possible. I am particularly indebted to some current residents of South Australia who have provided invaluable insights into the people and places you have recently read about. (See *Acknowledgements* next.)

While on that subject I feel I should qualify a few references: There are some fictional names and places included in the text, but these are very few in number. (Win and the Emporium at Glenelg are particular examples, as I never did get to know where my father found work there.) Some characters have been placed into the story to help interpret Mollie's experience for the reader, while others have been removed from the letters as their names would be irrelevant. But Hurtle and family and the Jacobson's were real people, and the dispute over money was sadly a key reason for the failure of my parents to settle in their Promised Land. As Hurtle's own sister Gladys put in a letter to Mollie after her return to English soil, 'If I'd been Eric I'd of sued him'.

This has been a very personal journey for me – the son who might have been a true Aussie if things had worked out differently! Sadly, my parents' story does not have the conventional ending you might expect in a novel: The Veale family returned to settle in Chorlton, and for a few short years they were very happy – especially (I like to think) when I was born in 1952. But in the years that followed my father's asthma was to worsen considerably. He finally lost his battle for life in December 1957, aged forty three. Mollie kept in touch with Helga Jacobson for a few years, and she too became a widow – but typically making a special effort to call on us in Manchester while on a visit to her relatives in Sweden. Susan and I never learned what happened to the sideboard...

Mollie died in 1985, aged seventy, only months after her older brother Alan. The following year my Auntie Elsie asked me if I would be interested in having some letters belonging to my mother. They had been kept safe in her own sideboard for over thirty years, and I cannot describe what it meant to me to read them for the very first time, as you have now done. I hope that Mollie's story has in some way touched you, or at least provided an insight into another world, in another time.

(You see? Finding those letters really *did* open a doorway to another land!)

# *Acknowledgements*

Having previously written a novel, I expected a work of nonfiction set around the lives of real people would be so much easier. I was wrong.

Putting myself inside my own mother's head, and trying to adopt the persona of a different sex in a strange country at a time before I was born has at times seemed a step too far. That I succeeded in completing this volume at all has been entirely due to help from sources too numerous to mention here. But I must mention the members of my writing group in particular: Alan Whelan, Ed Christiano (who also designed the front cover), and Mike Ward. Their feedback has often helped to steer me back on course, and I have delighted in the shared experience when we aired our mutual literary impressions over many months.

Some time ago I wrote to the secretary of the little church in Delamere SA, hoping to get some background to the local area. To my amazement that secretary (Linc Barrington) put me in touch with the local historian Lillian Cole – who was old enough to remember my mother in person! Both Linc and Lillian especially have provided material that helped enormously in painting detail on a unique historical portrait. They went to tremendous lengths to help me understand about life around Delamere, and about the farming community in particular. Much of the detail in Part Three is down to Lillian's personal knowledge, and the story of Peter Jacobson's car is entirely from her own memory! I am forever indebted to the Delamere residents (today and yesteryear) for all their help and friendship.

I am a married man, and I am truly grateful for my wife

Elaine being so supportive throughout the period in which I immersed myself in book number two. She it was who reminded me when to eat – and then put sustenance in front of me. She it was who tolerated my infidelity with the laptop, and she even played devil's advocate by reading extracts and considering the female perspective. I like to think we got it right between us.

My Big Sister Susan has always been there for me. The 'Little Imp' of this story has often surprised me with her memories of actual events – even from the viewpoint of a three year old. I am particularly grateful for her contributions of "The Night of the Storm" and Daddy's fire trick, for correcting me on the colour of the little leather handbag, and for passing a critical eye over each stage of the writing process.

Finally there are two people who I feel have guided me through the whole exercise: my mother and father. This was always about them. They were true pioneers in a world which seems so different to the one we know today. As a writer I have grown to realise that a novel works best when you let the characters lead you to the next part of the story. This work of nonfiction has been no exception, and I like to believe they have been there for me, guiding us all on an adventure that many more generations can now experience.

# Photographs & Illustrations

With the exception of those listed below, each of the photos is credited to Eric Veale:

*SS Esperance Bay*
old postcard

*Entrance to Southern Cemetery*
unaccredited on internet

*The Family Home*
Author's personal collection

*Arrivals at Elder Park Migrant Hostel*
SA Government Photographic Collection

*Keith Congregational Church in 1910*
unaccredited on internet

*Map of Glenelg*
Gregory's Street Directory of Adelaide & suburbs
(1949)

*Plans of South Australia*
drawn by the Author

All other graphics are reproduced from various souvenirs brought back on *Orcades*.
If anyone believes there has been a breach of copyright in reproducing any of the items in this publication they should contact the Author through his website
**www.alanveale.com**.

For a unique glimpse into Alan Veale's personal visit to South Australia in 2020 (just as the world was stricken by the coronavirus pandemic) read on for a short extract from his light-hearted travelogue ***Three Bears and a Jackaroo!***

(available on Amazon and also from Alan's website):

# THREE BEARS and a

# JACKAROO!

a light-hearted travelogue in Australia

ALAN VEALE

## Introduction

I'd waited over thirty years for this trip. Mum had died on 9<sup>th</sup> October 1985 at the tender age of seventy. Dad had passed away twenty-eight years earlier, aged forty-three. Up to that point, I only had a sketchy impression of my parents' experiences living in Australia before I appeared on the scene in 1952. Big Sister Sue was four-years-old when the Veale family left Adelaide in August 1950, so between us that particular period of family history was destined to pass from living memory.

Until Elsie gave me the letters.

Our aunt had been the recipient of over thirty letters written from Australia over a twelve-month period. These documented a fascinating story of two British Immigrants to South Australia, with their three-year-old daughter in tow, and their attempt to chase a dream. It took them by sea to Adelaide, then out to Keith, in the middle of what was once known as the Ninety Mile Desert. That was where their dreams fell apart, and they moved on to another remote spot on the Fleurieu Peninsula, before a further calamity brought them to Glenelg – and finally back to England.

In 2018 I transformed Mum's letters into a personal memoir I called *A Kangaroo In My Sideboard*, but it would be another two years before I finally had the opportunity to follow her footsteps, and to visit the places the Veale family had once tried to make their home.

This is that story, beginning in early March 2020 – just as a world pandemic was about to strike…

## The Three Bears, The Three Eighty – and the Aussie Cycling Team!

**Tuesday 3ʳᵈ March 2020.** I had a lot on my mind as I dragged the first case out to the car. Just after half past eight in the morning, a light drizzle and around 5 degrees Celsius. We had about an hour's drive ahead of us, so if we left by nine, we should be at the airport in plenty of time before our flight. I didn't want to leave anything to chance…

We'd even got new luggage – a matching set in burgundy that reminded me of Goldilocks and the Three Bears: Baby Bear, Mummy Bear and Daddy Bear. Elaine had done a fair job of loading most of her wardrobe into Daddy Bear, and as I lifted this 23.8 kilo heavyweight into the boot of the car, I realised there was no room left in it, even for Baby Bear! So, Mummy and Baby had to share the back seat – locked, stocked and labelled. We would be living out of these three for the next few weeks, so they were going to be treated with as much care as I and the airport baggage handlers could muster.

Driving to Manchester Airport was a familiar routine, joining the M6 motorway at Preston, then driving south to meet the M56 for the last part. Today the rain was persistent, and the traffic busy. My wife Elaine wisely kept her head in a book while I battled with the wipers and the speed merchants to get us safely through the first leg of our long, long journey.

But I did let one part of my brain ponder on how we'd come to this day.

Elsie gave me that bundle of letters some months after Mum died, in 1986. "You might like to keep these. I don't know why I kept them, but it makes better sense that you have them now." I had to agree with her. My mother's words would forever influence my feelings towards that land Down Under. I knew I would have to go there one day – but in the meantime I would go through two divorces and do my share of raising two children. Now my time had come.

Tomorrow I would finally set foot in Australia.

This was to be our first experience of the "Meet and Greet" parking facility. Normally, our holidays were just a week long, and we would leave the car in an off-site park before taking a shuttle bus to the terminal. But this was a special trip, and the car was to be left for over three weeks. All went smoothly, and within minutes of parking up we were wheeling the Three Bears into Terminal 1. Our flight would be Emirates E018, scheduled to leave at 13.10, and we were dropping off our bags at almost precisely the regulation three hours before departure. The girl on the desk was friendly and efficient, but not open to Elaine's enquiry about potential for an upgrade if the flight wasn't full... Oh well – we tried. Economy Class was sure to be a wonderful experience?

Walking through Security with minimal hand luggage was a novelty, and we only had Baby Bear and Elaine's small holdall for company. Our smallest case was a form of insurance: containing a few "valuables" and a change of clothing, just in case Mummy and Daddy Bear went Walkabout by the time we reached Adelaide. Could we be that unlucky?

We certainly felt relaxed and well-prepared once we'd passed the duty-free gauntlet. Time for a pre-flight drink, so while I was happy with one last pot of English tea, Elaine pushed the ~~boat~~ plane out with a couple of gin and tonics. At the appointed time we made our way to Gate 12, and had our first sight of the A380 aircraft that would take us to our stopover destination, Dubai.

I'd never flown in a wide-bodied jet before, and was amazed that this one even had an upstairs. We'd done our research (courtesy of Google) and selected seats at the pointy end, fairly close to the stairs up to Business Class, but away from the toilets and galley. The flight would be over seven hours, so we wanted to be as comfortable as our default Economy seats would allow.

We did find the experience quite pleasant, with just enough leg-room, and a complimentary pillow, blanket and headphones awaiting us. We had a seven-inch TV screen set into the seat in front, and a vast array of movies to choose from if we wished, while we charged our sundry devices from the adjacent USB port. (Okay, that's the end of the commercial for Emirates.)

Take-off was more or less on time, smooth and very quiet for such a huge airplane. I found it fascinating to follow our progress on the screen in front of me, where I could see outside through three different cameras positioned on the outside of the aircraft. There was also an option to monitor the journey with real-time graphics depicting our route across the globe, including altitude, airspeed and the time left to reach our destination.

The other thing of note had to be the meals. Anyone who flies long distance will tell you it's all about the food. The reason for this is not necessarily that what's on offer is of a particularly high (or poor) standard. It is simply that there seems to be so much of it! When you're sitting in one place for hours on end, trying to keep yourself occupied by watching back-to-back movies, or reading a book, the interruption of offers of complimentary snacks and/or drinks between meals is very welcome. So too are the meals themselves. The Emirates App I'd downloaded weeks before had provided details of the anticipated menus for lunch that we would receive, and soon after take-off the cabin staff handed out cards to confirm the choices available. In our case it was between Chicken Korma and Braised Beef, followed by Strawberry and Redcurrant Crumble. Proper metal cutlery came as standard, as well as a bread roll, coleslaw appetiser and a hot drink afterwards. All very welcome and well-presented – and quite tasty too.

Our flight to Dubai lasted around seven and a half hours, and we landed slightly ahead of schedule at around thirty minutes past midnight local time. Four hours ahead of the UK, we felt wide awake, and were happy to stretch our legs negotiating one of the biggest airport terminals in the world. The décor was impressive – marble, steel and glass, with a "cool" 23 degrees temperature and plenty of neon displays to inform the masses of our onward destination, or to encourage us to spend our dollars at any of the glittering displays of jewellery or high-class food outlets. Elaine was drawn to the former. (See above comments regarding food.)

With neither food nor bargain-basement jewellery to tempt us, the only pennies we spent were in the washrooms before passing through Security (again) to find our next gate for the longest part of our journey. The A380 had lived up to expectations, but the next leg was expected to be half as long again, through the night, and in an aircraft that could not boast an upper deck. How would a Boeing 777-200LR compare?

At the gate we got the first taste of new measures intended to cope with the spread of coronavirus. Until now, we had only seen one person at Manchester wearing a facemask. Here there were three officials with them on, and they were pointing temperature "guns" at our foreheads. A slightly intimidating experience, our discomfort aggravated further by being bodily padded down to check for weapons etc – but all in the interest of maintaining safety standards. It was about thirty minutes before our boarding time, and we found some seats away from the crowd, but soon there were plenty more joining us.

At this point I have to highlight a subtle difference between the two of us: while *my* strengths lie in the written word, Elaine can talk for England! And she's very good at it. In fact, Elaine's friendly nature towards people we met made the whole trip that much more enjoyable, opening up moments to treasure through conversation. Up until now our fellow passengers had largely appeared to be Brits flying on to other far-flung parts (as well as Australia), including one woman who told Elaine she was on her *seventeenth* trip to visit family in Adelaide. From this point on we would be getting to know some genuine Aussies.

Two men and two women sat on the seats in front of us, each of them clutching backpacks, and wearing identical black sports outfits. One of the backpacks had the name "Hayes" embroidered on it, and Elaine asked if they were on a cycling tour with Hayes Travel? "No," was the reply. "We're part of the Australian Cycling Team, and we're just on our way back from the World Championships in Berlin!"

Indeed, the four were soon six, each with a different name on their backpack, and then around another twenty made their way past the temperature guns and body-searches. We found that their performance at the Championships had not been particularly successful – but then Team GB had done even worse... These were true Aussies: friendly, cheerful and optimistic. The Olympics in Tokyo were beckoning in the summer, so there was plenty more for them to look forward to.

Suitably impressed by our first encounter with the natives, it wasn't long before we were called (in stages) to board our next aircraft, Flight EK 0440, leaving at 02.00 local time This time we were in the middle of the aircraft, getting a glimpse of the glitterati in Business Class as we walked through their compartment at the front to reach our seats. Not envious at all (!), we found a familiar collection of pillows, blankets etc awaiting our attention. In all respects the facilities of this aircraft were a good match for the A380, even down to the "starry" ceiling effect once the lights were dimmed for take-off. The difference this time was in our companions: A friendly Australian couple sat in the row in front of us, and immediately struck up a conversation, asking about ourselves and our plans. We told them the reasons for our visit, and they showed an interest, adding some recommendations for places to visit while we were in South Australia. They were from a town not far from Port Lincoln on the Eyre Peninsula, and they asked if we liked red wine. "Of course we do!" Their suggestion was to head to the Barossa Valley, and to look for a winery called Penfolds – a favourite spot of theirs. While we were chatting, two more cyclists sat in the row behind us – and then a third came to occupy the window seat next to me. All of them had big beaming smiles, and we were already beginning to recognise these as an Aussie trademark.

We faced a flight of between 12 and 13 hours, crossing the Indian Ocean with India and Sri Lanka to our left, and then nothing but sea below us for most of that time. Adjusting to the time difference was not easy. Having left Dubai in the middle of the night, I had expected we would soon be trying to settle down for whatever sleep we could manage. But our cabin crew had other ideas, and started to serve us breakfast within the first hour. It seemed slightly surreal to be eating a cheese omelette, croissant and coffee at 3 am local time, but I wasn't going to refuse it!

Sleep did come eventually, aided by ear plugs, an Emirates eye-mask, and our investment in a pair of special neck support/cushions that worked like a scarf wound tightly round the neck. I dozed on and off for a few hours, glancing at my screen one time to see a graphic of our plane flying over the ocean, but with the addition of a perfectly straight line crossing our path just ahead. It took a moment for me to realise this represented the equator, and instantly I remembered the passage in my Mum's memoir when *SS Esperance Bay* had done the same. The Crossing the Line ceremony had been a colourful occasion for all ships in those days, and I had imagined my Big/Little sister complaining that she couldn't see a physical line crossing the surface of the sea. Well, I could see it now!

The lengthy ocean stretch passed slowly but quietly, with the lights dimmed and most people either asleep or watching movies. I did watch a couple, but the experience seemed uncomfortable, the sound occasionally lower than I would like, and it was just something to pass the time. More memorable was the camera display underneath the aircraft, once we crossed the West Australian coastline exactly three hours before our scheduled landing in Adelaide. We flew above a terrain unlike anything I had seen before. The earth beneath was a rich combination of reds and browns, occasionally marked by yellow-ish streaks I assume were evidence of dried up river beds. Straight lines, indicating roads or railways, were a rarity – and townships of any size were completely absent. We might have been flying over the surface of Mars.

More food (of course), and sometimes animated conversation with our Aussie cyclist next to me. His name was Luke Plapp, aged 20, and a professional track and road cyclist from Melbourne. His parents lived there, but he had a base in Adelaide where he trained with his team-mates. He travelled a lot with them, and was looking forward to taking part in the Olympics in a few months' time. After listening to our own plans, he particularly recommended two beaches we should visit near Glenelg, at Brighton and Henley.

We landed with a bump or two, around twenty minutes early at 8.35 pm local time. We said fond farewells to our new friends, but the cyclists were still to make an impact on our progress. Border Control were masked up for virus prevention, and asked us if we had been to either China or Iran in the last 14 days? Realising it was a trick question, we both answered no. After safely collecting the Three Bears, we found ourselves in a lengthy queue behind two dozen Aussie cyclists as they meandered past more face-masked airport staff collecting immigration forms (we all had to complete them), with their special bikes boxed and crated in stacks on the luggage trolleys. One guy misjudged a corner (not medal-potential then) and yours truly helped him re-stack his load before we were able to escape into the warm Australian air and search for a taxi.

It was now around 9.15 pm, and our ultimate destination was the Glenelg Motel, about a ten-minute journey, so our taxi-ride was brief but door-to-door in a hybrid electric vehicle. The roads were quiet, and the fare twenty dollars (about £10). Undaunted by the gate preventing access to the motel, we and the Three Bears piled out in front of it. Anticipating our arrival "after hours", the proprietor Kylie had left instructions for us to find our key in a code-protected safe on the outside wall. Everything went to plan, the gate slid open, and humans and bears were soon wheeled inside chalet number 7. It was a large room containing two beds (one a single), an en-suite bathroom, wardrobe, settee and a desk. We also found a fridge and essential instructions to operate the air-conditioning.

We'd been a long time away from our bed back in England. But with an opportunity to get our heads down on some *proper* pillows for a few hours, it would soon be time for the real adventure to begin.

*Sorry, but that is the end of this Preview of*
***Three Bears and a Jackaroo!*** *by Alan Veale.*

If you would like to read the rest, then please visit the author's website for details on how to obtain a copy:
www.alanveale.com

# The Murder Tree

Published in paperback by Matador in October 2013

*It can be murder digging up your family tree, especially when your ancestor is trying to kill you.*

Chrissie Fersen desperately wants to know how she is connected to the death of a servant woman in Glasgow in 1862. Enlisting the aid of local librarian Billie Vane, she is determined to clear the name of the woman originally convicted of the crime. But her chief suspect appears to be alive and well – and it looks like he still has murder on his mind...

**The Murder Tree** introduces an unlikely pair of heroes: the

American daughter of a wealthy businessman and a Manchester-born librarian working in Glasgow. Each has their share of domestic strife to deal with, while sharing a thirst to find out the truth about a 150 year-old murder. But deaths are still taking place today as far afield as New York, and trying to dig through the roots of this unique family tree becomes more hazardous than either Chrissie or Billie could imagine.

*The Murder Tree* is based on the true story of Jessie McLachlan, convicted of murder in 1862, but who famously accused an old man of the crime after being found guilty at her trial.

Available in two formats:

Paperback ISBN: 9781783061112

eBook ISBN: 9781370494880

# The Titanic Document

*Publishing March 2021*

*It all comes down to who you can trust: the woman who got you sacked – or a killer from the British Government...*

- Powerful men kept secret what was really planned for April 1912
- Headlines of the disaster went contrary to expectations

- A mistake so huge it demanded concealment at the highest level. But the details survived through generations, causing panic for today's politicians

Peter Gris, Secretary of State for Northern Ireland, also sees his sexual perversions at risk of discovery. His actions to eliminate both threats mean tracking down and destroying historic evidence – and anyone who stands in his way.

*The Titanic Document* presents a thrilling new take on how the 1912 tragedy unfolded, as those tasked to keep the historical secret safe go on the run from an elite group of political figures.

*They sank the Unsinkable... but who planned the Unthinkable?*

Blending historical fact with an absorbing fiction that casts a cynical eye on politicians, *The Titanic Document* darkly observes the abuse of power and its consequences. *(ADULT THEMES)*

Further details are available on Alan's website: www.alanveale.com

Finally, if you wish to write to him for any reason, please use the contact form on the website, or message him through Facebook:

**@writetoAlanVeale**.

Printed in Great Britain
by Amazon

36621267R00126